THE CHURCH OF ENGLAND
Where Is It Going?

By the same author

_____

FOR
the staff and members
of Jesmond Parish Church
Newcastle-upon-Tyne

THE CHURCH OF ENGLAND

Where Is It Going?

David Holloway

KINGSWAY PUBLICATIONS
EASTBOURNE

ISBN 0 86065 365 X

Unless otherwise stated, biblical quotations are from
the Revised Standard Version, copyrighted 1946, 1952, © 1971, 1973
by the Division of Christian Education of the National Council
of the Churches of Christ in the USA

Front cover photo (Canterbury Cathedral):
I. Sharp, The Image Bank

Printed in Great Britain for
KINGSWAY PUBLICATIONS LTD
Lottbridge Drove, Eastbourne, E. Sussex BN23 6NT by
Richard Clay (The Chaucer Press) Ltd, Bungay, Suffolk.
Typeset by Central Southern Typesetters,
Eastbourne, E. Sussex.

Contents

Introduction

George Orwell first published his novel *Nineteen Eighty-Four* way back in 1949, just after the Second World War. In it he coined the word *doublethink*. *'Doublethink,'* he wrote, 'means the power of holding two contradictory beliefs in one's mind simultaneously, and accepting both of them.'[1]

True to form, 1984 was the year when some of the bishops in the Church of England came out publicly with the view that it was acceptable to 'doublethink' over the Virgin Birth and the Resurrection of Jesus Christ. They suggested that you could hold that Jesus was conceived by an act of human sexual intercourse, and that the remains of Jesus are still in the soil of Palestine: but at the same time you could stand up in church and say, 'I believe . . . He was born of the Virgin Mary . . . (and) On the third day he rose again.' Many were distressed. Many were confused. Some thought that unless some action was taken, at best this would split the Church of England and at worst lead to its demise as an effective Christian presence.

Reaction came from clergy in the north-east of England. For it was the new Bishop of Durham, the Rt Rev. David Jenkins who started the controversy. After his appointment but prior to his consecration he went on television and radio and appeared to be denying the Virgin Birth and casting doubts on the Empty Tomb. The Bishop of Newcastle then publicly defended him. And the Archbishop of York, in spite of requests for a deferment, went ahead with the consecration. It thus started as a problem for the northern province of York and the North-East in particular.

By the year's end, however, it was a problem for the whole Church of England with other provinces of the Anglican Communion throughout the world deeply shocked at what they took to be denials or doubts over fundamental Christian doctrines.

The consecration took place on July 6th 1984 in York Minster, one of the most famous and beautiful buildings in Europe. Three days later lightning struck the Minster and set its roof ablaze, causing enormous damage. Some saw this as the judgement of God and informed *The Times* accordingly. But the Archbishop of York flatly denied it (also in *The Times*), saying, 'What kind of a god do your correspondents believe in? . . . To interpret the effect of a thunderstorm as a direct divine punishment pushes us straight back into the kind of world from which the Christian Gospel rescued us.'[2] These remarks in themselves caused further theological furore!

Then there were a few quiet weeks of holiday. But, on September 3rd 1984 clergy in the North-East issued *The Position*. This was an uncompromising statement that 'enough is enough' (see Appendix 1). The debate had started in earnest.

This book is a continuation of that debate. The issues are still before the Church; and for the good of the Church they must be resolved.

David Holloway
Newcastle-upon-Tyne
Ascension 1985

PART 1

Setting the Scene

I

1984 and all that

In the year 2084 what centenary will Christian people be celebrating — that is if this inhabited planet survives?

Will it be the centenary of the death of David Watson, Anglican evangelist extra-ordinary; or the centenary of Billy Graham's country-wide campaign *Mission England*; or the centenary of the consecration of David Jenkins as a bishop in the Church of England after denying or doubting fundamental doctrines of the Creed?

In the Church *in* England these three men formed a focus for a range of concerns and interests during the year. But in one hundred years time, who will be remembered and who will be forgotten?

David Watson

The scene was York Minster (the roof was still intact). It was Saturday, March 17th 1984, the day for a great Thanksgiving Service for the life of Canon David Watson. On February 18th, a month earlier, he had died of cancer at the age of fifty.

He died relatively young after a life spent in the service of others. Those who sat in a packed York Minster on that cold March morning could not forget his remarkable gifts. Nor could they forget his own commitment to Jesus Christ. For

David Watson's great ambition was true 'discipleship' (the title of one of his best-selling books[1]). And he had lived what he preached. He took seriously Jesus' words:

> If any man would come after me, let him deny himself and take up his cross and follow me. For whoever would save his life will lose it; and whoever loses his life for my sake and the gospel's will save it (Mk 8:34–35).

He had lived a very simple lifestyle. He had made sacrifices of time, energy and money for the cause of Christ's kingdom and the growth of his Church.

But to see the significance of David Watson we really need to go back to the 1960s. It is not too much of an exaggeration to say that the sixties saw a turning point in British and then Western civilization. Old taboos and old restraints were being thrown overboard. Sexually, politically and even in the Church many were championing new freedoms. To others it often seemed anarchy. But no one could stop what was happening. It was a period of wealth and decadence.

It was also at this time that Bishop John Robinson published the book *Honest to God*,[2] in which he appeared to be questioning a number of basic beliefs. Before long others even more extreme were saying that 'God is dead'. The result? — the Church of England in many places lost its nerve.

At the same time, however, something else was going on, whose impact has yet to hit the nation and the wider world. In the universities there was a spiritual revival and it was associated with the growth of the Christian Union movement. This revival had begun in the fifties, but it grew significantly during the sixties and seventies. It was vitally important because a new generation of leaders was being influenced and shaped. David Watson was himself influenced by it and then was to help shape it. Its results will probably not fully appear until the 1990s!

But in all this David Watson's own ministry was developing. As a curate in Cambridge and then as a priest in charge of St Cuthbert's, York (a church which saw remarkable growth) he was to have more and more influence, especially on the younger generation. Indeed, his ministry to students was soon to be in demand all over the world.

Reminiscences

A number of us first experienced that student ministry on a Sunday evening in the early sixties. It was a meeting of the Oxford Inter-Collegiate Christian Union (OICCU for short). Students had packed into the Northgate Hall, Oxford, to hear a young curate from Gillingham, Kent. It was, of course, David Watson, recently ordained and in his first curacy. The lecture he gave was fresh and stimulating.

Perhaps one of his most effective student missions was in Oxford in February 1973 (which I witnessed as one of the assistant missioners).

How university missions were changing! There was now a folk singer before the main addresses in the Oxford Union (something never heard of before). There was a student 'drama group' (the forerunner of *Riding Lights* — the group later associated with David Watson in York). But most remarkable was the impact of the mission. It was estimated that each night of the week in February 1973 one in eight of the undergraduates of the university was present to hear David Watson. Oxford University as a whole was being influenced. The addresses of that mission, which were a masterly presentation of the gospel, have been written up as his book *In Search of God*.[3]

Soon after this David Watson developed his ministry beyond the student world to city-wide evangelistic festivals. The first big city-wide festival was in Leeds with the title *The Whole Story*. One of the side events of the festival was a theological debate with a professor of theology from Leeds University. The professor's name was David Jenkins. That was in 1977.

The following year, 1978, David Watson came to Tyneside for another city-wide festival, *Celebrate the Faith*. The City Hall in Newcastle was filled night after night: a large number of local churches of various denominations and traditions had joined in.

Another aspect of his work was his regular teaching at Fuller Theological Seminary, Pasadena in California. The seminary is well known for its School of World Mission with a whole department given over to church growth. David Watson took part in the seminary's continuing education programme where his courses on 'Church Renewal and Training the Laity for Ministry' and 'Evangelism in the Local Church' were always attended by large numbers.

But here we were, a huge crowd in York Minster, mourning his death. Our memories were different. But we were all giving thanks for David Watson's life.

However, the service of thanksgiving came to an end; and we had to step out into the cold air of the city of York. As we did so and as we stood outside the great West Door of that magnificent building, there was an odd sense that a new era was about to begin for the Church (or certainly for those parts of it David Watson had related to). David Watson had finished his course. New things would happen.

David Jenkins

The era, however, seemed to be having a problematic start! Television was not being very helpful to the Christian cause over the following few weeks — the Easter period. First, there was *Jesus – the Evidence*. This was a Sunday TV series and the result of eccentric scholarship. The series appeared to be based on the questionable assumption that secondary and later Gnostic documents were more reliable for constructing Christian history than the primary and earlier sources of the New Testament. The interpretation of the evidence held by many New Testament scholars in support of the traditional understanding of Christian origins hardly got a look-in.

But *Jesus – the Evidence* was nothing, in terms of its effects, compared with London Weekend's *Credo* programme scheduled a little later for April 29th, the Sunday after Easter Sunday.

The first I knew about this programme was a telephone call. 'What are you going to do about the statements of Professor Jenkins, the new Bishop of Durham?' asked the vicar of an Anglo-Catholic parish down the Tyne. (I then learnt that the Bishop-designate of Durham, David Jenkins, had been interviewed on the programme and apparently cast doubt on the Virgin Birth and the Empty Tomb of Jesus.) 'Nothing,' was my reply; but I added, 'if you intend to discuss these things with your PCC, you must first get a transcript of the programme and make sure you know what he really said. And get me a copy as well please.'

I thought no more about the professor (as he still was) from Leeds University. There were other things to think about. Billy Graham was coming to the north-east of England — to Roker Park, the home of Sunderland Football Club.

He was coming from Saturday, May 26th and would be there every night until Saturday, June 2nd. The North-East was integrated into the programme of country-wide evangelism and church growth called *Mission England* and so there was a lot of extra work immediately ahead.

Many people felt this was the chance of a lifetime. The veteran American evangelist was not likely to come again to our region; so we were all wanting to make the most of the opportunities.

But then, after a week or two, I received a transcript of the *Credo* programme. So what was all the fuss about? What had actually been said? Let me quote the relevant part of the programme.

'The Virgin Birth,' said the Bishop-designate in answer to the interviewer, Philip Whitehead, 'I'm pretty clear, is a story told after the event in order to express and symbolize a faith that this Jesus was a unique event from God . . . I wouldn't put it past God to arrange a Virgin Birth if he wanted to, but I very much doubt if he would.'

'So,' continued the interviewer, '[the birth narratives] don't amount to a historical record and shouldn't be seen as such, but as a series of stories to emphasize the unique importance of Jesus?'

'Yes . . . .' replied Professor Jenkins.

'Could we move on, then, now,' asked Philip Whitehead, 'to the most important miracle in the whole story of Jesus, the story of the Resurrection? Do you hold the view that Jesus rose from the dead and ascended into heaven?'

'Well,' said David Jenkins, 'I hold the view that he rose from the dead. The question is what that means, isn't it? I think I should like to say that it doesn't seem to me, reading the records as they remain in both the Gospels and what Paul says in 1 Corinthians, that there was any one event which you could identify with the Resurrection. What seems to me to have happened is that there were a series of experiences which gradually convinced a growing number of the people who became apostles that Jesus had certainly been dead, certainly buried and he wasn't finished. And what is more he wasn't just not finished but he was "raised up", that is to say, the very life and power and purpose and personality which was in him was actually continuing and was continuing both in the sphere of God and in the sphere of history so that he was a risen and living presence and possibility.'

Billy Graham

The transcript was put away in my file. I imagined it would never be looked at again. However, for anyone involved in *Mission England* it seemed more important that morning to read the newspapers to see what they had to say about Billy Graham.

He had recently arrived in the country and was due for his first series of meetings in Bristol. What was he going to be like after all these years? Some of us remembered him from 1966 and 1967 when he visited Earl's Court, London. I could also remember, as a schoolboy, his 'crusade' at Harringay,

London, in 1954. But was he going to be in touch with people in England in 1984? These were very different times.

The newspapers at this time were giving considerable coverage to religious affairs. However, this coverage showed that for many people questions of fundamental doctrine were of continuing concern. People were beginning to write letters about the views expressed on the *Credo* programme. Some like the Dean of Durham wrote in support. Others were opposed. It was obviously not only a vicar and a PCC of a parish on the Tyne that had been upset. There was concern around the country. And on Saturday morning, May 26th *The Times* had an editorial on the controversy.

But on Saturday evening of the same day, May 26th, hundreds of churches and chapels throughout the north-east of England forgot these things for the time being, for they were taking parties of people to hear Billy Graham in Sunderland.

The stadium had been well filled — in itself quite remarkable for a religious meeting in the North-East. Evangelistically, many reckon the region to be hard work. Billy Graham said it had been called 'the graveyard of evangelists'! Some of us feared that only 10,000–15,000 would be coming to the meetings. In the event it was more like 15,000–20,000 (an indication, perhaps, of how spiritually hungry people in the North-East are).

On that first night two things were of significance. First was the fact that those attending appeared to be a good cross-section of people. When Billy Graham gave his usual invitation ('I'm going to ask you to get up out of your seats'), punks jostled with the more well dressed, the young with the old, as hundreds moved forwards.

Secondly, it was significant that Billy Graham clearly had the ears of the crowd in spite of the weather — the evening was chilly from a wind blowing directly off the North Sea, and it included a sudden downpour of torrential rain. But he was very straightforward in his message; he preached a simple (but not simplistic) gospel.

Listening to the BBC's *Sunday* programme on Radio 4 the

following morning some of us, therefore, were waiting to hear about Roker Park. 'Ours is such a depressed area,' we thought to ourselves, 'with one-third of the industrial sector having to shut down over the last five years and a 20 per cent unemployment rate. Anything positive is newsworthy in such a context; so Billy Graham's 'first night' in the North-East is bound to be reported.'

But did we get a report on Sunderland? No! Not at all. Instead the main news item was on the Bishop-designate of Durham. And he was once again being interviewed about his beliefs.

BBC's *Sunday* programme

The discussion turned, naturally, to the subjects of the Virgin Birth and the Empty Tomb. The questioner, David Brown, said that the new bishop seemed to be saying that 'it is not essential for a Christian to believe in these as historical facts'.

To this the Bishop-designate replied: 'Well, that is absolutely right, because even if you did, no single historical fact can be certain. And secondly, no single historical fact can prove anything. I mean, historical facts are a matter of probability and doubt and uncertainty. Faith is to do with assurance that the people who bear witness to these facts have a conviction which we can share.'

'But isn't their inclusion in the New Testament, for example, evidence of certainty?' asked David Brown.

'Certainly not,' was the confident answer of David Jenkins. 'There is absolutely no certainty in the New Testament about anything of importance.'

We couldn't believe our ears. Not only so, but we couldn't help contrasting these doubts and this confusion with the clear preaching of Billy Graham the night before. At Roker Park we had a plain statement of the Christian faith as taught in the New Testament. It was preaching with the 'ring of truth' about it.

I suppose it was at this point that for me the controversy

went from the head to the heart. I believed something had to be done.

We were seeing some growth in the churches in the North-East. Our own church, Jesmond Parish Church, had grown to a Sunday attendance of 600; and other churches were also growing. People were being converted; lives were being changed; given time, this would have social and economic effects. There was no way that we could sit by and see someone come into the area from outside and undermine faith.

The announcer on the programme made it clear that concern was now widespread. He had said that these recent apparent denials of the reality of the Virgin Birth and the Resurrection had caused the *Church of England Newspaper* to declare that Professor Jenkins was not a Christian believer in the New Testament sense. 'He is,' affirmed the newspaper, 'a hindrance rather than a help to the people of God. He should not be allowed to take up his appointment as Bishop of Durham.'

The announcer also said that a nationwide petition had been instigated by the Chaplain of Hereford Cathedral School. It asked the Archbishop of York to invite Professor Jenkins publicly to affirm the Creed, and should the Professor refuse, the petition then asked the Archbishop seriously to question whether it was right to proceed with the Consecration. Obviously things were happening.

But one thing was noticeable. The people voicing protest did not include any members of the General Synod (the Church of England's Parliament). Why not? After all, the General Synod now has a large stake in the appointment of bishops. Its own Crown Appointments Commission submits two names of possible candidates for a vacant bishopric to the Prime Minister; and from these two names the Prime Minister in turn submits one name to the Sovereign.

Letter to *The Times*

At the end of Billy Graham's visit I therefore decided to

write to *The Times* myself, in my own capacity as a member
of the General Synod. The letter appeared on June 19th
1984.

Sir,
Clifford Longley has written (June 4th) very perceptively about
the views of Professor Jenkins, the Bishop-elect of Durham.

The nub of the problem relates to 'history'. On BBC Radio 4
recently David Jenkins said: 'No single historical fact can be
certain . . . historical facts are a matter of probability and doubt
and uncertainty . . . there is absolutely no certainty in the New
Testament about anything of importance.'

But all this is sheer nonsense! There are commonly agreed
criteria that can give us sufficient certainty about the past. It is
not 'probable' that D-Day took place on June 6th 1944; it certainly did. Nor is it 'probable' that Julius Caesar had an ex-
pedition to Britain in the first century before Christ; he certainly
did.

Professor Jenkins, in his *Credo* television broadcast, denied
that there was 'any one event which you could identify with the
Resurrection'. But in the duplicated letter he has sent out to
critics he said: 'I believe in the Resurrection in exactly the same
sense as St Paul believed in the Resurrection (i.e. on the basis of
the accumulated testimony of the first disciples and personal
experience).'

This is confused. David Jenkins is confusing *how* he (and St
Paul) came to faith with *what* he (and St Paul) believe. They
came, he says, to faith in the same way. But David Jenkins'
subsequent belief in the Resurrection and St Paul's are poles apart.

Paul believed that there was 'a datable event'. And Paul believed in the empty tomb: 'He was buried . . . he was raised on
the third day' (1 Cor 15:4).

Of that verse, C. H. Dodd, one of the greatest of English New
Testament scholars, has written this: 'The natural implication
would be that the Resurrection was (so to speak) the reversal of
the entombment.' And he adds: 'When (the early Christians)
said, "He rose from the dead," they took it for granted that his
body was no longer in the tomb; if the tomb had been visited it
would have been found empty. The gospels supplement this by
saying, it was visited and it was found empty.'

For these reasons is it right that David Jenkins should allow himself to go forward for consecration? We can't have bishops whose teaching undermines the truth of the Resurrection.

This is not to question for a moment David Jenkins' personal faith, or to deny that he has a real experience of the risen Christ. But a bishop has to be a person who can communicate the faith. He also has to lead with the good will and agreement of the Church.

At Professor Jenkins' consecration the Archbishop would have to say: 'Is it your will that he should be ordained?'

The people are to respond: 'It is.' What if a significant proportion were to say, 'It is *not*'?

Yours faithfully . . . .

I had stuck my neck out. But the response to that letter was quite remarkable. There were letters from all over the country, thus indicating that something very serious was happening or ought to happen. The proper course of action, it now seemed, was for a group of proctors (clergy on the General Synod) from the northern province of York to request the Archbishop of York to defer the Consecration. The matter could then be taken up in the General Synod. He refused the request, no doubt imagining that once Professor Jenkins was consecrated the problem would go away.

How wrong could he be!

2

Decline and growth

Jonathan Edwards, the great American theologian of the eighteenth century, said: 'The task of every generation is to discover in which direction the sovereign redeemer is moving and then move in that direction.' The experience of several continents at present indicates that it is not only a matter of faith but of fact that the Church is growing. Many are convinced that this is a significant work of God in the world of the 1980s. This is where they assume the energies of God's people need to be concentrated. Therefore, it is argued, we should be looking for growth in the Church of England.

Growth worldwide

The story and the statistics of what is happening around the world have now been documented by David Barrett in his massive *World Christian Encyclopedia* and by the Missions Advanced Research and Communication Center in the United States.[1] We can simply illustrate trends from three different areas.

First, there is Latin America. We can take the figures for the Protestant Churches in Latin America as they are clearer than for the Roman Catholic Church. In 1900 there were 50,000 Protestants. In the 1930s there were more than 1 million; in the 1940s there were more than 2 million; by 1970 there were 20 million; by 1980 there were 50 million. And at the same time we know that the Roman Catholic Church has also been experiencing a renewal in some places. The re-emphasis on the Bible, the charismatic movement and the development of basic Christian communities have all affected the Roman Catholic Church.

Second, there is Africa. In 1900 there was one Christian for every 28 non-Christians in the continent. By 1975 there was one Christian for every 2.5 non-Christians. As an illustration of what is happening, the Church in Kenya has grown over this period from 5,000 to 8 million!

Third, there is the Far East. In Indonesia the annual church growth rate is 10 per cent. South Korea is experiencing even greater growth. In 1966, 11 per cent of the population was Christian; in 1978, 19 per cent; in 1981, 22 per cent. Church growth in Korea, a predominantly shamanistic country, is now proverbial. Just after Billy Graham left England in the summer of 1984 he visited Seoul, the capital, and spoke to a gathering of one million people in Yoido Plaza (and that was at the same time as transport was limited: half the cars were off the roads because of petrol rationing). In 1982 I had the opportunity of being present at the Full Gospel Central Church in Seoul, one of the most remarkable churches in the world. 8,000 people were at a Friday all-night prayer meeting when I arrived. On Sunday more people attended worship than are present at Wembley Stadium on Cup-Final Day! Not far away was the Young Nak Presbyterian Church, with 60,000 meeting for worship. The largest Methodist Church in the world is also in the same city, as are many smaller churches. And the Full Gospel Central Church is still growing. In 1982 it had 18,000 home 'cell' groups. In 1984 there were 21,000.

It was Bishop Stephen Neill who was concerned that we had right assumptions with regard to the growth of the Church in the world. He wanted to challenge the assumption that worldwide the Church was in decline. He refuted the view that 'the Christian percentage of the world population has already begun to decrease and will continue to grow less till the end of the century.' As an able scholar and missiologist he concluded that the percentage of Christians throughout the world 'has been slowly increasing since the beginning of the century.' Because the Church is growing worldwide he made the observation that never in human history has there ever been what might be classified as a universal religion, until today. But now 'for the first time there is in the world a universal religion, and that the Christian religion.'[2]

So why do so many people assume that the Church is in decline? Simply because we look at the Church from the perspective of Western Europe and from the perspective of the British churches in particular. Therefore, when we are asked the question, 'Where is the Church going?' we are tempted to reply: 'Nowhere, only down!'

Decline in the Church of England

The sad fact is that in the United Kingdom *all* the mainline denominations are in decline.

The Church of England's figures in this respect are important and symptomatic. It must be remembered that Anglicans account for 38 per cent of Church members in England and Wales (Roman Catholics 33 per cent and all others 29 per cent). Figures for the Church of England show decline. The long-term decline in membership seems to have resumed after six years when numbers appeared to plateau. Confirmations dropped in 1981 and 1982. This was the first significant fall since 1974.

Confirmations declined from 190,000 in 1960 to 80,000 in 1982. In the north-east of England recent figures[3] show an *annual decrease* in confirmations of 5·2 per cent for Durham and 7·2 per cent for Newcastle. Each year of course there are fluctuations, but the overall picture is one of downward drift.

It is true that over the five years 1980–85 only a 5 per cent fall-off in terms of membership of electoral rolls is predicted.[4] But this figure is probably accounted for by the fact that throughout the Church of England, besides there being over-all decline, there are many churches that are growing vigorously.

But decline is not new. It has been going on for more than a hundred years. An easy way to understand the situation is to compare the Parliamentary *Census Report of 1851* on 'Religious Worship' with *Prospects for the Eighties,* from a census of the churches in 1979 undertaken by the Nation-wide Initiative in Evangelism. They both give us figures for Sunday worship.

According to the *Census Report of 1851,*[5] on Sunday March 30th 1851 there were just under 11 million attend-ances at the various churches. As some went twice, the stat-isticians of those days came up with a figure of 7,261,032 people out of a population of just under 18 million who had been in church at least once on a Sunday, that is 39 out of every 100 of the population were in church.

But according to *Prospects for the Eighties,*[6] in 1979 there were only 11 out of every 100 of the population in church (18 out of every 100, however, were Church members — on membership lists or electoral rolls). On Tyneside and in Sunderland it was as low as 9 out of every 100 in church on any given Sunday.

The seriousness of this is especially evident when we con-sider that the young are now at risk spiritually. The chances of them having an intelligent presentation of the gospel of Jesus Christ are diminishing. With declining churches young people are often not being presented with even the funda-mentals of the Christian faith in an adequate and appropriate way. In the North-East this is true both of rural areas and of urban areas.

An informal survey in 1978 in an area of rural Northum-berland near the Scottish border showed that there was vir-tually no specific Christian work being done among *teenagers*. Yes, there was *younger children's* work, but no Bible study or discussion group for young people at the top end of the school system.

We might excuse this as being a rural problem. But in Newcastle it is not much better. The Royal Grammar School, Newcastle-upon-Tyne, takes boys in its Senior School from 11 to 18. After Billy Graham's visit to Roker Park one of the masters put a question to the boys in the 'Inters' section of the school Christian Union (20 boys in the 13–14 age bracket). They were asked how many of them were in churches where there were other people of their own age. Only three put up their hands.

Decline after growth

Before we proceed further we need to ask this question: isn't there something inevitable about decline after a period of growth? Should we, therefore, be too worried in the Western World? Aren't there cycles of 'confidence and confusion'? Is one generation so 'over-confident' in what it believes that the next generation has to ask radical questions, thus causing confusion and decline?

There is a theory that church growth occurs when people on the 'fringe' of churches become more committed or are converted. But complete 'outsiders' hardly get touched. In a great revival, therefore, people totally outside the influence of the Church do not replace the stock of people who become more committed. In time this pool of potential 'converts' dries up! Growth then stops; discouragement sets in; faith is weakened and decline occurs.

If this is true in the British Isles, it may not point to any *inevitability* of decline. Rather it may be pointing to the lack of any effective 'cross-cultural evangelism' — something we in this country are notoriously bad at. Those completely outside the Church ever since the industrial revolution have not only been distanced from the churches in terms of what they believe, but also in terms of culture and social class. What is needed, therefore, is a strategy of evangelism that addresses itself to this fact. The key, as we shall see later, is probably to be found in 'church planting' and finding appropriate 'bridges' for growth.

This problem is related to John Wesley's observation of the way decline often sets in after growth. He says it is because spiritual revival leads to an improvement in living standards and material prosperity. Riches lead people away from God!

Here are Wesley's words:

> Wherever riches have increased, the essence of religion has decreased in the same proportion. Therefore, I do not see how it is possible, in the nature of things, for any revival of religion to continue long. For religion must necessarily produce both industry and frugality, and these cannot but produce riches. But as riches increase, so will pride, anger, and love of the world in all its branches . . . Is there no way to prevent this — this continual decay of pure religion?[7]

Donald McGavran, the pioneer writer on church growth, has coined the phrase 'redemption and lift' for this phenomenon:

> Over two or three generations, redemption and lift separate Christians from their social roots and seal off whole denominations from the lower classes. When that happens, churches cease to grow.[8]

So a period of 'church growth' poses its own special problems. But these problems can never *justify* decline.

Doctrinal confusion and decline

One of the fundamental causes of church decline is theological. For it is now clear beyond doubt that church growth and doctrinal confusion are mutually incompatible. This is one of the reasons why the Church of England cannot afford to have any of its senior leaders causing doctrinal confusion; and, therefore, that is why it cannot have its bishops, by their action or inaction, declaring belief in the Virgin Birth and the Empty Tomb to be optional in the Church.

In 1972 Dean Kelley's book *Why Conservative Churches*

are Growing was published in America.[9] It was a very important study and it caught the attention of the American religious public in a big way, such that a new edition was soon called for. This was interesting since the book was essentially a sociological rather than a theological work. Nor was it written from the perspective of a conservative Christian. Dean Kelley has been an executive of the National Council of Churches in the United States, a body often associated with a theologically liberal stance. But during a period of sabbatical leave, Kelley looked into the whole field of church growth, and his conclusion was simple: theologically liberal ideas and views aid church *decline;* they do not aid church growth.

Kelley starts off by showing that the mainline religious denominations in the United States as a whole are in decline, but many individual churches are growing. His concern was to find out why.

Here, we can only summarize his argument. His basic premise is that the main function of religion is to answer fundamental questions about the meaning of life and society — 'What are we here for?' 'Is there a God?' 'What happens after death?' 'Is there a "right" and "wrong"?' Religion, therefore, is a supplier of meaning. And lack of meaning is dangerous, because a society can disintegrate without a uniting set of values and understandings. If it cannot find meaning to life, its citizens often turn 'to unproductive or even destructive activities, including crime and addiction.'[10]

However, in 'liberal' churches there is often a 'neglect of meaning' in the interests of social and political action. Such liberal churches 'abdicate their unique and essential contribution to healing the world's wounds — *meaning.*'[11] Few then find these churches attractive or relevant. Conversely, the more 'conservative' churches and churchmen that are clear about what the gospel is and so provide a framework of meaning meet needs and find that their churches are more likely to be growing churches.

Kelley is not advocating pietism. This does *not* mean

that the religious group's business is 'spiritual' or 'sacred', and that it should leave material, temporal, secular affairs to those who — allegedly — understand them better . . . The subject matter of religion is *the entire life of human beings and whatever affects them*. But the distinctively religious treatment of that subject matter is not technological so much as *meaning-orientated — how can life be understood, its meaning perceived, developed, celebrated and enhanced*.[12]

We may not agree with every word of Dean Kelley's analysis. But this hard fact remains: it is the theologically conservative churches that are growing. Theologically liberal churches or, to use Kelley's words, 'ecumenical churches', are declining.

Theological assumptions and perspectives

Both growth and the role of the Church in God's plan need to be defined to avoid misunderstanding. Eight simple points can be made.

First, God is establishing his kingdom. The great evidence for this is the Resurrection of Jesus Christ. The Empty Tomb of Jesus is to be seen not just as an isolated miracle, proving that God exists! It is rather part of the total plan of God in history. That plan was put into effect with creation and will be consummated at the end time. The apostle Paul writes of God's 'purpose which he set forth in Christ as a plan for the fulness of time, to unite all things in him, things in heaven and things on earth' (Eph 1:9–10). And speaking to the Athenians, Paul said:

> The times of ignorance God overlooked, but now he commands all men everywhere to repent, because he has fixed a day on which he will judge the world in righteousness by a man whom he has appointed, and *of this he has given assurance to all men by raising him from the dead* (Acts 17:30–31).

Second, the kingdom of God is bigger than the Church; and the Church is bigger than the Church of England (or any other denomination or quasi-denomination such as a house church grouping).

It is true that there are different views about the relationship of the Church to the kingdom. Howard Snyder's thesis is this:

> The Church gets into trouble whenever it thinks it is in the Church business rather than in the Kingdom business . . . Church people think about how to get people into the Church: Kingdom people think about how to get the Church into the world.[13]

P. T. Forsyth argued that 'the *State* is an agent of the kingdom of God, the Church is the kingdom of God *in the making.*'[14] But whatever the precise relationship is between the kingdom and the Church, this fact remains: if the Church in a given locality becomes non-existent or too weak, there is nothing, and no one, to get into the world to work for the kingdom or to be in the process of 'making the kingdom'!

Third, the Church is thus vital for the kingdom; we can call it the '*primary* agent' for the kingdom. This means that the Christian is released from the burden of individualism and of having to act on his or her own. Yes, God's work in the world is to be done by individuals *but* acting together as the 'body of Christ'. The term 'church growth' reminds us that there is a corporate dimension to Christian work, witness and evangelism. However, although the Church is the primary agent, it is made up of fallible people who are being changed into God's likeness. We therefore do not look for perfection this side of eternity.

Fourth, God is causing his Church to grow and it is only *God* who gives the growth (cf. 1 Cor 3:6–8). However, God uses people to achieve his purposes; so a Paul or an Apollos helps with the work of growth. Paul plants and Apollos waters. But not all growth is God's growth. There are, indeed, tares as well as wheat growing in the harvest field! And as in nature, pruning is sometimes required to generate strong growth.

The complexity of growth

Our fifth point is that the growth of the Church involves many factors. As with the human body growth occurs *when all the parts — very different parts — are working together and working properly* (Eph 4:15–16).

Growth is thus multidimensional: it involves both personal spiritual growth and growth in numbers. It involves both growth in the quality of fellowship and growth in a transforming interaction with society. And there is no one magic formula: for example, if the Church of England sorts out its doctrinal confusions, confusions highlighted by the new Bishop of Durham, it will not automatically grow. There are many other considerations. *But if the Church of England tolerates doctrinal confusion, that is one factor that will prevent growth.*

Sixth, growth does not in one sense occur by trying. As Jesus pointed out, you cannot grow taller simply by trying. You cannot say, 'Now I am going to grow.' No, you must make sure that the factors for growth are present (health, food, sleep etc) and then you will grow. There needs to be an environment for growth.

The seventh point is more sociological. In 1979 I was able to study a number of growing churches in different parts of the world. I noted five factors present in all of them, or five dimensions to the environment of each one.

One: there was a *vision* of what God could do through the church.

Two: there was *believing prayer*. These churches did not just talk about prayer: they actually prayed.

Three: there was a *concern for the Bible*. This is not to say that all the churches would have agreed over every aspect of biblical interpretation. But they all submitted to its authority.

Four: there was *strong leadership* exercised by a senior pastor, but at the same time it was a *shared* leadership. The senior pastor was no mere executive of a church committee; his leadership was properly delegated.

Five: there was *social and structural awareness*. That is to say there was an awareness about the basic social and structural realities of the church *and* of the world around. There was an awareness of how organizations work. They seemed to realize that no organization, least of all a church, can function unless four conditions are met.

Our eighth point is to identify these conditions. There has to be one, an agreed agenda; two, competent leadership; three, enabling structures; and four, an awareness of and an interaction with the (social) environment. Indeed, James D. Anderson and Ezra Earl Jones say that

> for ministry to function at an optimal level, all four components must be correlated. The process of ministry breaks down when any one of the four components of ministry is overlooked or subordinated to the others.[15]

PART 2

Doctrinal Arguments

3

What does the Church of England believe?

We have seen that church growth and doctrinal confusion are mutually incompatible. But what does the Church of England really believe?

It will here be helpful to talk about the Anglican 'package' of beliefs, for belief is more than a set of isolated propositions; it also includes attitudes.

Anglican belief can be 'unpacked' and seen in terms of at least nine elements.

The Bible and liturgy

First, there is the *biblical basis* for the whole life of the Church of England. Bishop Stephen Neill, writing this time not about church growth but about Anglicanism, writes of:

> the *biblical quality* by which the whole warp and woof of Anglican life is penetrated. At every point the theological appeal is to Scripture. Article VIII of the Thirty-nine Articles tells us that the Creeds are accepted and recited because they may be proved by 'most certain warrants of Holy Scripture'. The Anglican Churches read more of the Bible to the faithful than any other group of Churches.[1]

So being a biblical Church, the Church of England rejects what it sees as traditions contrary to Scripture in the Roman Catholic Church; but unlike some other Protestant Churches it sees nothing wrong in traditions and practices that Scripture seems to have no particular view about. It does not hold that everything has to be positively licensed by Scripture before it can be introduced into the Church.

The essence of the Anglican approach to the Bible is, therefore, this:

> Show us anything clearly set forth in Holy Scripture that we do not teach, and we will teach it; show us anything in our teaching and practice that is plainly contrary to Holy Scripture, and we will abandon it.[2]

Second, the Anglican Church is *liturgical*. It believes that a form of service in worship is consistent with the freedom of the Holy Spirit, who can work through that form. But the Anglican Church is not rigidly liturgical, as has been evidenced by the introduction of new and modern services. Unlike some of the free churches there is, however, an instinctive caution about liturgical change. The opening words of 'The Preface' to the Book of Common Prayer make the point:

> It hath been the wisdom of the Church of England ever since the first compiling of her Publick Liturgy, to keep the mean between the two extremes, of too much stiffness in refusing, and of too much easiness in admitting any variation from it.

Because the Church of England is liturgical, the Creeds feature very prominently in worship.

Catholic, established and episcopal

Third, there is an awareness that the Church of England is *continuous* with the Church before Henry VIII. The Reformation in the Church of England was precisely that — a 'reformation' and not a new start. The Church of England is thus felt to be one with the apostles, the early Fathers and the great medieval saints (in the north-east of England these were men like Aidan, Cuthbert and the Venerable Bede).

The Church of England is felt to be, therefore, the *Catholic* Church in England. Elizabeth I wrote in 1563 to the Emperor Ferdinand:

> We and our subjects, God be praised, are not following any new or foreign religions, but that very religion which Christ commands, which the primitive Catholic Church sanctions, which the mind and voice of the most ancient Fathers with one consent approve.[3]

Fourth, the Church of England is *established by law*. Canon A.1 *(of the Church of England)* makes just two observations about the Church. First that it is 'established' and secondly that it is 'apostolic': 'The Church of England, *established according to the laws of this realm* under the Queen's Majesty, belongs to the true and apostolic Church of Christ' (italics mine).

Let us clarify this. The establishment is often understood as referring to the *effects* of the establishment — the fact that bishops sit in the House of Lords and the Church of England enjoys other apparent privileges. But the establishment is fundamentally an establishment 'according to the laws of this realm'. The state has accepted the Church of England as a Christian body and given to it a certain legal position. Further, the Church of England is under 'law'. This does not imply any legalism, it is just a fact that during its history, the Church of England has evolved a way of settling disputes and regulating its affairs 'according to the laws' which then bind the Church corporately.

But these church laws are not immutable. They can be changed through constitutional means which now involve the General Synod, the major law-making body of the Church, with Parliament still retaining a 'veto' in some cases.

Fifth, the Church of England is *episcopal* — it has bishops. There are different views about bishops. Some believe they are of the *esse* of the Church (they are essential). Others believe they are of the *plene esse* of the Church (they are not essential, but the Church is deficient when you don't have them). Yet others believe that bishops are of the *bene esse* of the Church (they are not essential; it is better to have bishops than not; but the Church is not *automatically* deficient without them). This last group, of course, denies the validity of the gibe that you can be a good Anglican if you believe in episcopacy, no matter how much else you may disbelieve!

Comprehensiveness

Sixth, the Church of England is *comprehensive*. Since the Reformation and the Elizabethan Settlement there have been three emphases within the Church. First, there is the emphasis that Scripture must always be paramount and never neglected. Secondly, there is the emphasis that the historic teaching and tradition of the Church should be remembered and not forgotten. Thirdly, there is the emphasis that God-given reason has its proper place in the life of the Church.

Within the Church of England these three emphases have coexisted, happily or unhappily for centuries. But this coexistence has been possible because there has been agreement over fundamentals.

Classic expression of these fundamentals is given by a great sixteenth-century Anglican, Richard Hooker (c.1554–1600). He taught that certain things are non-negotiable. These formed what he called 'the very essence of Christianity'. Yes, secondary matters of doctrine and practice were negotiable, but not this essence.

This 'essence of Christianity' contained three elements, Hooker said.

First, we have to 'name the name of Jesus Christ' and confess him as Master and Lord. 'Christians, therefore, they are not,' says Hooker, 'which call not him their Master and Lord.'

'But,' he continues, 'our naming of Jesus Christ the Lord is not enough to prove us Christians, unless we also embrace that *faith,* which Christ hath published unto the world.'[4]

The second element, therefore, in this 'essence of Christianity' is the apostolic faith; it is no good just saying you believe in Jesus! There has to be content to that belief; and he defines what is the minimum of this content of faith by referring to the 'rule of faith' in the early Church Fathers, Tertullian and Irenaeus. This rule was an early 'Creed', very similar to the Apostles' and Nicene Creeds. So Hooker makes it clear that the Christian 'faith' is not just an attitude of heart but must include 'those few articles of Christian belief'. 'Those articles' are more or less the clauses that make up the two Creeds said regularly in the Church of England.

The third part of this 'essence of Christianity' is baptism. You have to submit to the outward rite of baptism, a rite ordained by Jesus.

So Hooker argued that there should be unity with any Christians who 'named the name of Christ', believed the clauses of the Creeds, and were baptized. He liked the fifth verse of Ephesians 4: 'one Lord, one faith, one baptism'; this summarized the fundamentals of Christianity for him. These were non-negotiable. But over secondary matters we should tolerate differences of opinion, and that would mean a degree of comprehensiveness.

Down the centuries that has been the Anglican position — agreement over fundamentals and toleration of different views over lesser issues.

One of the most recent statements on comprehensiveness in the Church of England was in 1968. At the Lambeth Conference that year one of the reports put it like this:

> Comprehensiveness demands agreement on fundamentals, while tolerating disagreement on matters in which Christians may differ without feeling the necessity of breaking communion.[5]

Some leaders of the Church today, however, seem to be redefining comprehensiveness. They are defining it as a dialectic of mutually contradictory views. Thus, for example, it is possible for some to believe, and others not to believe, that the remains of Jesus are still in the soil of Palestine. Both beliefs, they maintain, witness to the truth. But such a view of comprehensiveness is not the historical Anglican position.

Tolerance and its limits

The seventh element in the Anglican 'package' is that the Church of England is *tolerant, but within limits.* Comprehensiveness in the Church of England inevitably leads to tolerance over certain beliefs or practices that would be considered mutually exclusive in other churches. But there is a point at which the Church of England, in effect says, 'Thus far and no further.' There is a place for intolerance in the Church of England.

During the Reformation period the Anglican Church was intolerant of those who insisted that episcopacy must be replaced by a presbyterian system. It was intolerant, as we shall see, at the time of the Deist controversy in the seventeenth and eighteenth centuries of those who believed in God but not really in revelation.

But perhaps the most interesting case of corporate Anglican intolerance or 'limitation' of doctrine occurred in the last century.

John Henry Newman (1801–90) is one of the most remarkable figures of English Christianity. He was a godly, brilliant Oxford scholar and a great Church politician. He lived at a time when the Church of England had lost the biblical doctrine of the Church. Some, in those days, simply saw the Church of England as another department of government! So Newman and the Oxford Movement, of which he was a leader, tried to revive the biblical teaching on the Church. 'It is "the Body"; it is "the Bride"; it carries the authority of Jesus Christ, its divine head; and the gates of Hell will never prevail against it,' they were reminding the rest of the Church. However, the only way to save the Church of England, Newman taught, was to get back to the purity of the Catholic Church — a purity lost at the Reformation. And to spread these ideas Newman and his friends published *Tracts for the Times* (hence their nickname 'the Tractarians').

But Newman's views were changing fast. Like his friend Richard Hurrell Froude, he could say, 'I am every day becoming a less and less loyal son of the Reformation.' And in 1841 he wrote *Tract 90.*[6]

This was Newman's look at the Church of England's Thirty-nine Articles. Written at the time of the Reformation, these Articles were an attempt, after various arguments and debates, to reach a consensus. They are less rigid than some of the other Confessions of the same period, and indeed less rigid than the Westminster Confession of English Presbyterianism. But they are clearly Protestant and Reformed. After all, Article XIX says this:

> As the Church of Jerusalem, Alexandria, and Antioch, have erred; *so also the Church of Rome hath erred, not only in their living and manner of Ceremonies, but also in matters of Faith.*

Newman and common sense

Newman argued that 'the Protestant Confession [the Articles] was drawn up with the purpose of including Catholics, and Catholics now will not be excluded.' He may have been right, he may have been wrong, but that is not the point. The point is that it was Newman, the casuist, writing. He had too subtle a doctrine of the Catholic Church. And when he said the Articles were drawn up to include Catholics, you couldn't be sure he didn't mean Roman Catholics who were giving allegiance to the Pope. It was a brilliant tract, but it went against the Anglican way of doing things.

The preamble to the Articles gives us this Anglican way:

> No man hereafter shall either print, or preach, to draw the Article aside any way, but shall submit to it in the plain and full meaning thereof: and shall not put his own sense or comment to be the meaning of the Article, but shall take it in the literal and

grammatical sense.

If Newman was right, he first should have shown beyond doubt that his interpretation was the common-sense or straightforward interpretation.

For the Church of England cannot, nor ever has it, ultimately allowed 'black' to be called 'white' or vice versa. Newman had actually gone too far for the Church of England. The Bishop of Oxford, Bishop Bagot, said:

> I cannot persuade myself, that any but the plain obvious meaning is the meaning which as members of the Church we are bound to receive; and I cannot reconcile myself to a system of interpretation which is so subtle, that by it the Articles may be made to mean anything or nothing.[7]

This approach of the bishop is being *straightforward or not devious*. And that is the eighth mark of the Church of England. It is this desire neither to be devious nor to fly in the face of commonsense that is both offended and bewildered by the *doublethink* among bishops and theologians. For, as we have seen, some on television or in one of the other mass media say they do not believe in the Virgin Birth of Jesus and doubt his Empty Tomb, but then stand up in church and recite the Creed, saying 'I believe . . .'. Apart from seeming to be dishonest, this is to reject a basic aspect of the Anglican tradition. This offends. For it is an assault on the plain meaning of words. And in the Anglican Church 'the plain obvious meaning is the meaning which as members of the Church we are bound to receive.' If this was so with the extremely subtle arguments over the Articles, how much more is it the case with the Creeds!

Newman, ultimately, realized he had no long-term place in the Church of England, and he eventually joined the Church of Rome — maybe that was providential, as some of the reforms taking place today in the Church of Rome are due to his influence.

If the Godly Newman had no place, surely, some bishops have no long-term place *as bishops* in the Church of England.

These are those who by 'a system of interpretation which is so subtle' can make the Virgin Birth and the Resurrection on the third day 'mean anything or nothing'. For the Church of England is committed to being straightforward and not devious. It is committed to common sense and reason.

Yes, Scripture is the primary authority. The Church must listen to the witness of the past. But the Christian faith must be shown to be reasonable by the criteria of historicity, coherence and common sense.

A 'middle view' of the Church

The ninth element in our 'package' is having *a middle view of the Church*. Newman on the one hand and some Independents on the other hand could be said to have a 'purist' approach to the visible Church. But, as we have seen in Article XIX, the Church of England believes that the visible Church can 'err'.

The Roman Catholic tradition tends to deny that there can ever be important doctrinal error in the Church. The Independents (including some in the modern house-church movement) fully admit error in the Church, but proceed to form new churches. They argue that such error invalidates a church.

But the Church of England is more pragmatic. It notes that the churches of the New Testament were far from being inerrant. Indeed, many of the books of the New Testament were written to correct doctrinal errors in churches. The Church of England therefore believes that the visible Church is not perfect, while believing equally that the visible Church throughout the centuries has not been totally apostate! Since the Holy Spirit guides the Church, the Church should therefore be expected to reach truth in some of its tradition.

The Church of England has taken seriously the criterion for belief of Vincent of Lérins (died before 450): *quod ubique, quod semper, quod ab omnibus creditum est* ('what has been believed everywhere, always, and by all'). That is why it accepts the three Creeds from the early centuries of the Church's life. These have come from the consensus of the Church and, as we have said, 'they may be proved by most certain warrants of holy Scripture' (Article VIII).

For this reason the Church of England does not accept the position, often advocated by the cults that eighteen hundred or nineteen hundred years of Church history have been off-centre. Nor does it accept the Roman position that all has been well (at least in the Roman allegiance).

And this is why there is a suspicion of those who say that for eighteen hundred years the Church has been wrong over the Virgin Birth and the Empty Tomb. On the other hand there is also a suspicion of those who say that *everything* that has ever been taught about the virginity of Mary and the bodily Resurrection is automatically correct.

According to the Canons

In the light of this 'package' of Anglicanism, we can now ask: 'What does the Church of England believe according to its Canons?'[8] For constitutionally this is where we have the doctrine of the Church of England defined.

The doctrine of the Church of England is spelt out in Canon A.5. The *Church of England (Worship and Doctrine) Measure 1974* (5.1) makes it quite clear that this is the Canon above all Canons for defining Anglican doctrinal statements. Nor is this some ancient text from the Reformation period. The new Canons were agreed during the fifties and sixties and came into force as recently as 1969.

Canon A.5 says:

> The doctrine of the Church of England is grounded in the holy Scriptures and in such teachings of the ancient Fathers and councils of the Church as are agreeable to the said Scriptures. In particular such doctrine is to be found in the Thirty-nine Articles of Religion, the Book of Common Prayer and the Ordinal.

But how do we interpret this Canon A.5? Two points need to be kept in mind.

First, in terms of Church Law (and the Canons form part

of the law of the Church of England) the Canons have to be considered as norms; and therefore they have to be interpreted strictly *until* they have been proved otherwise, by the courts.

Second, we must be careful about the word *grounded*. The words *grounded in Holy Scripture* are not to be taken to mean 'So long as the origin of a belief can be shown to have started in the holy Scriptures anything goes. A belief is permissible as Anglican doctrine therefore, even if it is now a flat contradiction of the beliefs taught in the Scriptures.' No! For these words are to be taken as meaning 'The Scriptures are *foundational* (at the ground level)' and so the doctrine of the Church of England *at least* includes these authorities as sources; but others are not precluded. There might be more; but the Scriptures and the teachings of the Fathers and councils that agree with the Scriptures are normative and determine the legitimacy of anything else. Indeed, the Canons themselves are 'other authorities' for the Church of England and they need this sort of 'enabling'.

Now it is clear beyond a shadow of doubt, from both common sense and legal advice, that the Virgin Birth (more accurately the 'Virginal Conception' — we, however, will refer to the 'Virgin Birth' for short) and the Empty Tomb of Jesus are taught in all these authorities mentioned in Canon A.5.

It follows that to deny the Virgin Birth and the Empty Tomb (or to declare them optional) in the Church of England is uncanonical. Such a denial goes against the teaching of the Canons of the Church of England. Furthermore, bishops along with the other clergy have sworn solemn oaths of obedience, swearing in effect to be bound by the Canons.

Error

A bishop, however, is under a stricter obligation than the other clergy. For he is also under Canon C.18. Section 1 of C.18 says:

> Every Bishop is . . . to uphold sound and wholesome doctrine, and to banish and drive away all erroneous and strange opinions;

and to set forward and maintain quietness, love, and peace among all men.

'Wholesome doctrine' has to be defined by Canon A.5. So bishops who deny or declare optional the Virgin Birth and the Empty Tomb are doubly in defiance of the Canons because of Canon C.18 as well as A.5. And that is a serious matter. It is not that the Canons are infallible; there are constitutional ways of changing the Canons. But if corporately the Church has decided that it accepts these doctrinal Canons, what does it say for the integrity of the Church when a number of its bishops reject them?

The Church of England does believe that there is such a thing as heresy. The modern Canons understand that there are 'erroneous and strange opinions'. This is only following the Book of Common Prayer, in itself a doctrinal standard for the Church of England.

At ordination in the Book of Common Prayer, the question is put to both those being ordained as priest and those being consecrated as bishop: 'Will you be ready, with all faithful diligence, to banish and drive away all erroneous and strange doctrines contrary to God's Word?' In the new Ordinal the question is similar but simpler: 'Will you . . . uphold the truth of the Gospel *against error*?' At the revision committee of the Alternative Service Book's new Ordinal there was hot debate as to whether the phrase *against error* should be included. It was voted in, and subsequently passed by the whole General Synod! The Church of England most recently has, therefore, decided that while 'heresy hunting' is certainly not now the way of the Church of England, there is such a thing as 'error'. And that has to be opposed when it manifests itself. And heresy when paraded has to be attacked.

From all this it seems that without doubt the Church of England, as a corporate body, is committed to a belief in the Virgin Birth. And it is committed to a belief that the tomb of Joseph of Arimathea was empty on that first Easter morning, not because of theft but because God raised Jesus Christ from the dead.

4

Today's world and the Virgin Birth

How is it that now several among the Church's senior leadership seem to be forsaking, if not subverting the Anglican tradition? Is it that the Virgin Birth and the Empty Tomb are simply false? Perhaps at last we have bishops who can lead us from 'simple believism' into the brave new world of the twenty-first century. This obviously is a possibility.

Nothing new under the sun

But how brave is the new world? And are those who believe in the Christian fundamentals (as plainly taught in the Bible) naïve believers?

There is a simplistic assumption in some quarters that in the nineteenth century the gulf between the Bible and modern man was finally established; and so modern theologians have to take people across that gulf. This means, first and foremost, that Christian doctrine has to undergo a radical reappraisal and revision.

Every age forces us to rethink. But there is an arrogance about the modern age: there is a belief that now things are so new and so different that all previously held convictions and assumptions have to go.

Christopher Booker sums up this state of mind in these terms:

Just as few adolescents can ever believe that their parents have been through the same stages of attitude and development before them, so one of the more frequently recurrent fallacies has been people's belief that their own age is without precedent, that some new order is coming to birth in which all the general assumptions previously made about human behaviour are becoming somehow outmoded. In few ages has this belief been more prevalent than our own.[1]

But it is always wise to look at historical parallels before assuming any behaviour or beliefs are new. We then often discover that 'there is nothing new under the sun' (Eccles 1:9).

Critical doubts about the Bible go back to almost Bible days. And they remind us that such doubts come from different world views rather than inherent problems in the text of the Bible. The great struggle in the early centuries was between the orthodox Christians on the one hand, and between various 'Gnostics' on the other hand. That is to say, it was between those who held the biblical view that God could really involve himself with the 'stuff' of creation (this material and messy world), and between those who said God was a great 'mystery' beyond all knowing; and he certainly wouldn't get involved with virgin births!

In the early centuries Cerdo, Cerinthus, Saturninus, Carpocrates, Marcion and the Manicheans denied the Virgin Birth from this Gnostic position. Some, like Cerinthus, followed the Jewish Ebionites who said that Joseph was Jesus' natural father. But Marcion explained Jesus' origins by saying that a supernatural being came down directly from heaven in the fifteenth year of Tiberius! (And to make life easier for himself, Marcion was cavalier with the New Testament. He rejected the opening chapters of Luke!)

Over the centuries there have been many critical doubts. If we move to the seventeenth and eighteenth centuries we find Deists who deny the Virgin Birth. Then in the nineteenth century there was the much publicized denial of the Frenchman, Ernest Renan, in his *Life of Jesus,* published in 1863. Although Bishop Gore was able later to damn the book with faint praise ('an exquisitely conceived and executed romance rather loosely or remotely based upon history'), it caused an enormous sensation at the time.

The denial of the Virgin Birth is nothing new. Unbelievers have long denied the Virgin Birth. What is new is that we now have *bishops* in the Church of England openly denying or doubting it.

Early problems with science

But someone says: 'Ah, but it *is* different today. Never before have we had such a revolution in our thinking about the physical universe and what can or cannot happen in nature. Science has made all the difference. We *must*, therefore, revise our doctrines.' But is that so?

Too many people are unaware of the philosophical and scientific background to the New Testament world. We know from the biblical records that thinking people in the Graeco–Roman world of those days were attracted to the outlook of the Epicureans or the Stoics. When Paul went to Athens, 'Some also of the Epicurean and Stoic philosophers met him. And some said, "What would this babbler say?"' (Acts 17:18) — a not too friendly reaction!

The belief system behind the Epicurean and Stoic schools of thought had come from the earlier Greek philosopher Democritus. So Epicurus, like Democritus, claimed that all existence is matter. Ultimately there are atoms and void. He was particularly concerned to discredit the idea that God could be involved in managing the world. Gods are 'higher' than we are; but they cannot break natural laws. The Stoics also held an 'atomic' theory of the universe, in such a way that every event was caused by some other event 'according to natural law'. Everything was determined.

In these circles there was a vigorous belief in the power of 'science'; and this had implications for religious belief. In the century before Christ (only as distant from New Testament times as the nineteenth century is from us), Lucretius wrote passionately in an attempt to destroy religious superstitions. He was a popularizer of the views of Epicurus.

Notice how he speaks of his 'hero' liberating people with 'science':

> The vital vigour of his mind prevailed. He ventured far out beyond the flaming ramparts of the world and voyaged in mind throughout infinity. Returning victorious, he proclaimed to us what can be and what cannot . . . *Therefore superstition in its turn lies crushed beneath his feet, and we by his triumph are lifted level with the skies.*[2]

Whatever the merits of these ideas, they were intellectual currency in New Testament times. To think that modern man is in a unique position because of science is itself a myth. We must not assume, therefore, that we have automatically to 'rethink the gospel'. It was in a sceptical context that the gospel of Jesus Christ was often first preached.

And we need to note that Luke's Gospel (which contains a full account of the Virgin Birth and the Empty Tomb) seems to be meant for cultured Romans.

An early response to science

Science and philosophical questioning have always been factors in the background of Christian thinking. Sometimes they have been more significant than at other times. But the gospel has always been preached against the backdrop of one 'world view' or another since the time of the apostles. Quite often it has to challenge that world view.

The first major scientific development after the apostolic age came in the second century. There were new developments in astronomy at Alexandria in Egypt. Ptolemy clarified and published the ideas of Hipparchus of Nicaea on how the planets move in space. Ptolemy's theories were very sophisticated: in the *Almagest* (1.5) the conclusion was reached that 'the earth, in relation to the distance of the fixed stars, has no appreciable size and must be treated as a mathematical point.' And this was in the second century!

But did the Christian Church then revise its doctrine (as some now advocate) or react (as it did with Galileo)? No! The greatest minds in the Church realized how provisional even the best scientific descriptions are.

Basil of Cappadocia not long afterwards in the fourth century, discussing Genesis chapter 1, produced a very practical if somewhat cynical philosophy of science — nor is it totally irrelevant for today:

> Natural scientists and philosophers have attempted to 'explain' nature; but not one of their theories or systems has remained firm and unshaken; each is overthrown by its successor. *Refutation is thus unnecessary.*[3]

Indeed, that is the approach today of many Christians who are scientists towards certain scientific theories or models. Use them when they are useful for practical purposes; but be careful of thinking that they are giving you *absolute* truth about the nature of reality.

None of this, of course, disproves the assertions of some of the bishops and theologians who deny or doubt the Virgin Birth and the Empty Tomb. Rather it just acts as a warning light. It makes us hesitate before thinking that our age is so different and that we really have to revise the gospel.

However, we must address ourselves to the problems connected with the Virgin Birth of Jesus. First of all, of course, we must admit that in the hierarchy of truths the Virgin Birth is less central than the bodily Resurrection of Jesus. Further, we know that in the early centuries the interest in the Virgin Birth was on the *birth* (the fact that Christ was genuinely born) as well as on the nature of his conception. But none of this allows us to ignore the conception and say the *Virgin* Birth doesn't matter!

The Virgin Birth and the Bishop of Durham

In the *Durham Lamp* (the Diocesan Newsletter) for December 1984 the new Bishop of Durham wrote about the

Virgin Birth. He entitled his article 'Christmas and the challenge to faith'. Various things were argued for.

He argued for the need to understand symbolism.

> It must be clear to both ourselves in our belief and to any neighbours in their unbelief that — unlike, say, stories about Father Christmas — these Christmas stories are told 'for real'. Now this is where all the trouble and distress arises for some people . . . . They simply cannot understand, or simply will not listen to, the point that many of the stories of the Bible are 'for real', not by being literally true, but by being inspired symbols of a living faith about the real activity of God. But if you really believe in a real God, then you simply have to be able to use, and know something about *symbols*. For no statement about God is simply literally true.

So the Bishop's conclusion is this:

> We have no right to insist on the literal truth of the story about the Virgin Birth . . . We have every right to give clear and convinced thanks for the obedience of Mary . . . We have no right (and no need) to insist on literal angels . . . We have every right to give thanks to God for the way he sends his messengers to men and women . . . We have no right to insist that the stories like those about the Shepherds and the Wise Men are verbatim historical accounts. But we have every right — and a clear calling — to insist that faithful Israelites and searching Gentiles did discover, and do discover, through the leading of God . . . that He is with us as Jesus Christ and through His Spirit.

But what are the grounds for these assertions? Two reasons are given. First:

> Everyone knows that a good story loses nothing in the telling. This is clearly true about the story of Christmas. Cribs and animals and winter snow and much else have been woven as imaginative embroidery around the stories of the birth of Jesus from a very early stage, with each generation or century adding its bit.

And second:

> Virgin birth stories are not unique to the founder of Christianity

and there are really very serious critical and historical grounds for treating that story as one of the very early embroideries around the wonder of the discovery that this Jesus is God for us.

What, then, is the Bishop saying? First, that you have to use 'symbols' in talking about God; and 'virgin birth' stories are appropriate 'symbols'. Second, he is saying that legendary material attaches itself to these sorts of accounts. Third, he claims that the Virgin Birth is paralleled in other religions and traditions. Fourth, he argues that 'serious critical and historical grounds' must make us reject the Virgin Birth as 'non-fact'.

New Testament evidence

Let us deal with the last point first. Does the critical study of the New Testament mean we have to reject the Virgin Birth? And are there 'historical grounds' for rejecting it?

The traditional view of the New Testament evidence is summed up by John Stott in a sermon he preached at All Souls', Langham Place, London. This was a rejoinder to episcopal denials of the Virgin Birth.

> The narratives of Matthew and Luke have the same core. Both attribute Mary's pregnancy to the Holy Spirit not Joseph, and both write of the perplexities of the chief actors regarding her virginity. But their accounts are independent (there is no evidence of collusion) and complementary (their perspectives are different). Luke describes the angelic Annunciation to Mary, and *her* perplexity as to how she could become a mother when she had no husband. Matthew describes Joseph's discovery of her pregnancy, and *his* perplexity, his resolve to divorce her because the child was not his, and his dreams in which God told him to take her to his home and marry her. Thus, Luke tells Mary's story, and Matthew Joseph's. Ultimately, the facts must have come from them, whether in written or in spoken form. Since Luke spent two and a half years in Palestine, while Paul was in prison there, it seems very likely that he obtained his story from Mary direct. At all events, the evidence is that we have in the New Testament two genuine, early, separate accounts of the

Virgin Birth, each independent of the other, and each comple-
menting the other, the one going back to Mary and the other to
Joseph.[4]

Here then is the main evidence of Matthew and Luke. But
in addition there are hints in the other Gospels that support
their evidence. Some contemporaries of Jesus seem to have
been suggesting irregularities in his birth (Jn 8:41; 9:29).
And Mark, who does not explicitly refer to the Virgin Birth
(he begins his account of Jesus with the baptism), calls Jesus
the 'son of Mary'. The other Gospels call Jesus the 'son of
Joseph' or the 'son of the carpenter'. Mark never does. But
to refer to Jesus as the 'son of Mary' is strange. It suggests
something irregular, if not illegitimate, about the birth of
Jesus. Sons were not called by their mother's name unless
paternity was uncertain or unknown.

All this, then, is the traditional and common-sense interpretation of the evidence. But what could someone admit
who took a more 'critical' approach?

Raymond E. Brown takes such an approach and sums up
his view of the accounts of the Virgin Birth like this:

> It seems clear that the two evangelists traditionally known as
> Matthew and Luke, writing in the era A.D. 80–100, believed that,
> in conceiving Jesus, Mary remained bodily a virgin and did not
> have intercourse with Joseph — they were not consciously pre-
> senting us with a theologoumenon. Neither evangelist knew the
> other's infancy narrative, and the fact that a virginal conception
> through the power of the Holy Spirit is one of the few points on
> which they agree means that this tradition antedated both
> accounts. Indeed, it had been in circulation long enough to have
> developed into (or to have been employed in) narratives of a
> quite diverse character and to have circulated in different Chris-
> tian communities.[5]

But that is very significant, because once we admit that
the Virgin Birth itself is not a *late* embroidery and has 'been
in circulation long enough to have developed' its own tradition, we are back into the time of 'living memory', as we

will be discussing later. And we must remember that the infancy narratives are clearly of Palestinian origin. They reflect Jewish fears of Herod the Great and Jewish piety focusing on the Temple worship in Jerusalem. But James, Jesus' brother, became the head of the Church at Jerusalem. He was, therefore, in a position to correct any Palestinian traditions where they misrepresented the facts, or were pure fiction; and he was in a position to give 'family' information if required. After the Resurrection it is only reasonable to assume that James, now converted, talked with Mary about Jesus!

Parallels with other religions

If all this is so, why reject the New Testament evidence? There must be other strong reasons for believing that this material is legendary or 'embroidered'. So what about the claim, made by the Bishop of Durham, that 'virgin birth stories are not unique to the founder of Christianity'?

On investigation it seems that the Virgin Birth is unique. You do not find a 'virgin birth' paralleled elsewhere.

First, as Alan Richardson, a Professor of Theology and then Dean of York, says quite bluntly: 'There is no real parallel to the story of the birth of Christ in pagan literature.'[6] It is true that marvellous births have been credited to figures in world religion and in Graeco-Roman mythology. But these instances usually involve a type of 'holy marriage' where a god, in human or some other form, impregnates a woman, either through normal sexual intercourse or through some other substitute *sexual* means.

There is, of course, the argument that the early apologist Justin Martyr (c.100–c.165) first used, that crude and mythological divine-human unions are merely shadowy pointers to the cosmic reality of the birth of Jesus from the Virgin Mary. But even if that were true, the Virgin Birth of Jesus is still very different from these pointers. To say they are parallels is most misleading.

Second, there is no parallel in Hellenistic (i.e. Greek-speaking and Greek-influenced) Judaism. Someone may be asking: 'But couldn't the Gospel writers have got their ideas from Hellenistic Judaism? Doesn't Matthew quote the Greek text of Isaiah 7:14: "Behold, a *virgin* shall conceive, and bear a son, and shall call his name Immanuel"? Perhaps the Virgin Birth was "invented" from this verse?'

The answer to this is 'No!', for there is no evidence that in Hellenistic Judaism this verse in the Septuagint (the Greek version of the Old Testament) was ever taken to refer to a 'virginal' conception. The verse simply can mean that a girl who is now a virgin will conceive (in a natural way). Of course, once Matthew knew of the event of the Virgin Birth, he could look back to the Greek Old Testament and see how this verse 'fitted in' and was fulfilled in what had happened. But before the time of Christ this verse was never linked with the Messiah's birth.

Third, there is no parallel in 'mainstream' Palestinian Judaism. There was no expectation that the Messiah would be born of a virgin. Nor is this at all surprising. Natural sexual relations for a Jew would have been quite acceptable and totally appropriate as a means for God to do a new work through a special anointed person.

The parallels, if we can call them that, lead us 'away' from the idea of a Virgin Birth. There was an existing tradition in the Old Testament of special children being born with divine intervention; but it was through natural human intercourse. This happened in the case of Isaac, Samson and Samuel. These are Old Testament parallels. But they bear no likeness to 'virgin births'.

The contrast is seen in Luke himself. He records the birth of John the Baptist as special in the Jewish way: his parents were aged and barren, and God intervened. But the account of the birth of Jesus in Luke is totally different. John's birth was all of a piece with the Old Testament instances of God enabling the barren to give birth to children he had promised. But the birth of Jesus is without parallel. If someone had been inventing a birth story about Jesus we would expect it to have been along these Jewish lines. But the birth story of Jesus is not along these lines! It is very misleading, therefore, to say that 'virgin birth stories are not unique'. The birth of Jesus *is* unique.

Legends

David Jenkins also says that good stories 'lose nothing in the telling'. That is correct. After the Gospels were written, the Christmas stories attracted legendary material down the centuries. But no one is suggesting that this legendary material is part of the Gospel account!

However, four things need to be said as we assess the assumption that the Virgin Birth is itself legendary.

First, it is quite true that the Gospel account has no reference to animals around the manger. Such a suggestion is a later tradition, based not on the New Testament but on a doubtful reading of Isaiah 1:3 by later enthusiasts. We could add that the Gospel accounts do not mention Father Christmas or Christmas trees!

But the issue to discuss is not the paraphernalia of Christmas nor legendary accretions; but *whether there was something there in the first place to generate all these 'poetic' traditions*. Matthew and Luke says there was: the birth of Jesus from the Virgin Mary.

Second, the simplicity of the biblical narratives contrasts profoundly with all the extra-biblical embellishments that have accumulated over the centuries. There is no evidence at all that Matthew and Luke are themselves generating stories. For example, the story of the visit of the Magi and the slaughter of the infants of Bethlehem in Matthew is entirely in keeping with what we know from elsewhere of Herod the Great.

Third, the accounts in Matthew and Luke have an authentic ring about them; they are distinctly Jewish. They come from the world of ordinary Jews with their Jewish marriage customs. They come from the world of Jewish piety — the world of Zechariah, Elizabeth, Simeon, Anna, and Joseph and Mary themselves. They do not read like legends.

Nor, fourth, can we say that while not being legend, the Virgin Birth is something of a 'tall story' or parable. It is quite true that Jewish rabbis sometimes used 'tall stories' and parables to make points. But Matthew and Luke knew all about this, for as they make quite clear in their Gospels, Jesus was a master of this art. But Matthew and Luke knew when Jesus had *stopped* telling 'tall stories' or parables. The Jews knew fact from fiction, and the Virgin Birth is reported as fact not fiction!

There do not, therefore, seem to be strong arguments for 'imaginative embroidery' being used by Matthew and Luke, as the Bishop of Durham suggests. How then can he claim that there are 'really very serious critical and historical grounds' for rejecting the Virgin Birth? Perhaps the real problem is philosophical. As he said on the original *Credo* programme: 'I very much doubt if God *would* arrange a Virgin Birth.' But Christianity (certainly at the point of the Incarnation) is concerned with what actually happened. We cannot rewrite history to fit in with our presuppositions!

This brings us to the question of symbolism, which we will deal with in our next chapter. In the meantime we can go along with Jerome who once said: 'We believe that God was born of a virgin because we read it!'

5

Symbolism and the Empty Tomb

Deism was a heresy that threatened the existence of the Church of England in the eighteenth century. But what precisely was Deism? Like early Gnosticism there were many varieties of it. 'Probably we need do little more than characterize it as "belief in a non-interventionist God".' That is how the Oxford theologian, David Brown, defines it.

He goes on to argue that

> in striking contrast to German theological thought which with the decline of Bultmann's influence and the rising star of Moltmann and Pannenberg has moved in a more conservative direction, it is not difficult to find prominent exponents of deism within contemporary English theology. Nineham's *The Use and Abuse of the Bible* and Wiles' *The Remaking of Christian Doctrine* might be taken as representative examples.[1]

We may note that it was the Rev. Professor Dennis Nineham who was invited to preach the sermon in York Minster when the Archbishop of York consecrated David Jenkins as a Bishop of the Church of England, three days before the Minster roof was destroyed by fire.

However, for the moment we will forget Professor Nineham and focus only on the Archbishop of York and the Bishop of Durham and what they say about symbolism and history. For some of *their* recent pronouncements have also been criticized as being deistic.

York Diocesan leaflet

In July 1984 the Archbishop wrote in the *York Diocesan Leaflet* about the Virgin Birth as being a 'symbol' of the Incarnation (God becoming man). The Virgin Birth is 'a fitting expression of this truth,' he said: 'the most important point is that, for the purposes of Christian faith, it is what a doctrine tells us about God that matters, rather than whether it is possible to make firm historical judgements about an event which is by its nature inaccessible to ordinary investigation.'

Of course, symbols are used in the Bible, for example, in the book of Revelation. But is the Virgin Birth essentially a *symbol* of the Incarnation or uniqueness of Jesus? Does the Bible indicate that and do the early Fathers of the Church indicate that?

First, there is no evidence in the Bible that the Gospel writers would have chosen to express the uniqueness or sonship of Jesus in terms of a Virgin Birth. Luke clearly sees the Virgin Birth as *leading to* the holiness and sonship of Jesus. But there is no evidence that Luke saw the Virgin Birth as *proving* holiness and sonship. And Matthew had other interests. Matthew puts the 'primary emphasis on answering calumny, on affirming Davidic descent and on fulfilment of prophecy,' as Raymond E. Brown reminds us.

Second, if the New Testament age generated the Virgin Birth narratives as a symbol of the Incarnation, it was singularly unsuccessful. In the early centuries, the Virgin Birth had a bad track record. For it led to considerable speculation and confusion.

The early Christian Fathers simply took the nativity accounts as given and then saw points of application for their own needs. What is conspicuous is how crudely they did this. Ignatius sees the 'star that shone in the East' as being the cause of the downfall of witchcraft![2] Justin sees the Virgin Birth as the true fulfilment of the immoral actions of the

Greek Gods![3] Ambrose saw the Virgin Birth as the call to celibacy![4] And both Ambrose and Augustine saw it as a sign of the sinlessness of Jesus because his conception was not tainted by sexual intercourse![5]

It is obvious that the Incarnation does not *demand* the Virgin Birth — hence the bishops who deny the Virgin Birth but say they believe in the Incarnation — for the Virgin Birth does not *prove* the Incarnation. But if that is so, why would the Gospel writers have used the story of the Virgin Birth in the first place?

The easiest answer is 'because it happened'. It is not that the Virgin Birth is essential for the Incarnation: it is that given the Incarnation, the Virgin Birth is thoroughly believable. We cannot, therefore, say that the Virgin Birth is the Incarnation's symbol. The record in the New Testament of the conception and the birth of Jesus is precisely that — a record of the conception and birth of Jesus!

But is the Empty Tomb a symbol of the Resurrection?

Easter in Durham

In his April 1985 Diocesan Newsletter, the *Durham Lamp,* the Bishop of Durham seemed to suggest that the Empty Tomb is a symbol of the Resurrection. It is a symbol of

the assertion, made by God and received by faith, that in this world, through this world and beyond this world we may be sure that in the end, love succeeds, love brings it off, love has the last word. Jesus, the flesh and blood expression of down-to-earth love is at the very 'right-hand' of God.

After talking like this about the *meaning* of the Resurrection of Jesus from the dead, the Bishop went on to suggest that on that first Easter Sunday morning the tomb of Jesus may not really have been empty after all.

Answering the question 'Was the tomb empty?' the Bishop wrote:

Maybe it was, maybe it was not. As is now, perhaps alas, notorious I personally do not know whether the grave was empty or not. The evidence of the texts, the nature of the tradition and the general facts about the way people all over the world rapidly believe appropriate stories to support their religious beliefs leave me wholly uncertain about the Empty Tomb as literal historical fact.

But, of course, the man in the street is not impressed. He thinks that if the remains of Jesus are still in the soil of Palestine, that has disproved the whole thing. Christianity will have to be relegated to the realm of aesthetics. It is only a pretty story — perhaps the prettiest story ever told. But it is not fact. He knows you can't prove the Resurrection true with mathematical certainty; faith on good evidence, he realizes, is probably where you start; but he is totally convinced that you can in principle *falsify* the Resurrection. If the remains are still in the soil of Palestine, that, sadly, is that! The Resurrection has been proved false.

So there was a public outcry over Easter, 1985. The old Bishop of Norwich and the new Bishop of Peterborough were calling for the resignation of the Bishop of Durham. 'Doubting bishops' were in the news again.

The content and grounds of faith

The Archbishop of York wrote to *The Times* on April 10th to defend such doubting bishops. He made two points, one simple and one more complicated. First, he argued that the content of faith must be distinguished fromt the grounds of faith (what you believe is different from why you believe it); but then, secondly, he wrote this:

> The content of faith, though substantially grounded in history, transcends its historical grounds. It is not a bare recital of events, but the recognition of certain events, stories, images and experiences as being *revelatory of God.*

It doesn't matter, he went on, about the detailed facts of history 'providing there are sufficient historical grounds for asserting *that revelation has indeed taken place*' (italics mine).

This is the problem: 'the content of faith' *sometimes* 'transcends its historical grounds'; but *not always*. Let me explain.

Besides distinguishing the content of faith from the grounds of faith, we have to distinguish something else. We have to realize that this content of faith (all that Christians believe) covers two types of belief at last. It covers not only belief about God's being and nature *in general,* but it covers also belief about God's purposes and actions *in particular* instances of history. So the meaning of Easter is indeed 'that God does indeed act to bring life out of death' and that 'love succeeds, love brings it off and love has the last word' and 'love is at the very "right hand of God"'. But those *general* trus only hold good because of the *particular* intervention of God in raising Jesus Christ from the dead on the third day and leaving a vacant tomb!

The content of the Christian faith, thus, includes both general truths about God *and* accounts of his particular interventions in history. It is belief about his person *and* his direct work, for the Christian believes that God is a 'God . . . who gives life to the dead' (Rom 4:17) in general *and* that 'God raised him [Jesus] from the dead' (Rom 10:9), in particular.

But the logic of what the Archbishop of York and the Bishop of Durham have been saying is that Christianity is fundamentally about *out knowledge of God in a general way*. Even in God's actions in the world are so that 'revelation takes place'. Of course, if that were so, it wouldn't matter whether what is 'revelatory of God' is a real event or a myth. So long as your mind is informed and you have correct ideas about God, that is the heart of the matter; it is then up to you. But is that what Christianity is fundamentally all about?

The gospel, as the Bible teaches it and the Church Catholic has understood it over the centuries, is this: in Jesus Christ God *did* something. He didn't just teach us lessons about deity; in Jesus Christ something cosmic literally *happened.*

In the life, death and Resurrection of Jesus, God's kingdom was inaugurated. The new age began. So Jesus and especially his Resurrection are about *fulfilment* and *change* — with practical consequences. They are not just about receiving *gnosis* ('knowledge').

And that is why the historical facts, including the Empty Tomb, matter. They do indeed tell us something about the being and nature of God, but we cannot reduce Christianity to an experience or knowledge of the Divine. The good news, the gospel, is that God has done something to affect the universe, whether we understand it or not. The gospel is that reality has changed. And that doesn't depend on us.

So the gospel according to Jesus was: 'The kingdom of God is at hand' and according to the apostles, 'Jesus and the Resurrection'. The gospel is, therefore, about God *and* history, not just about God alone. That was the lesson the Gnostics could not understand in the early centuries of the Christian era, nor the Deists in the eighteenth century. It is a lesson, surely, the current leadership of the Church of England must grasp as a matter of urgency.

The Empty Tomb and the evidence of the texts

But perhaps the Empty Tomb is fiction. Perhaps, therefore, it can only be a symbol of something more general? Perhaps God and the material world don't meet. Perhaps the Gnostics were right! Perhaps we can't be sure that God acts on the plane of history. We can only have knowledge of a God 'up there'.

The Bishop of Durham wrote in his Easter 1985 newsletter that he was clear about the problems of the Empty Tomb. They are threefold. First, there is 'the evidence of the texts'. Second, there is 'the nature of the tradition'. And third there are 'the general facts about the way people all over the world rapidly believe appropriate stories to support their religious beliefs.' This is why the Bishop is '*wholly uncertain* about the Empty Tomb as literal historical fact.'

Space prevents any detailed consideration of the Resurrection. For a detailed treatment of the New Testament issues see Murray Harris, *Raised Immortal* (Marshall, Morgan and Scott, 1983); for a general treatment see my *Where did Jesus go? — the truth and meaning of the Resurrection* (Marshall, Morgan and Scott, 1983).

However, we must make some comments about the Bishop's reasons for doubting the Empty Tomb. The first reason he gave in the *Durham Lamp* was the textual evidence.

The main textual evidence for the Empty Tomb, however, is in the Gospel narratives. Unlike the Virgin Birth, which has only limited coverage in the New Testament, the Empty Tomb is in all four Gospel accounts. So why reject it? The argument sometimes put forward is that the Resurrection accounts are all so different. But is that a good enough argument? No! For there are a number of factors that lead us to accept the narratives *on their own terms,* without even the support of the evidence from the Epistles and the Acts! Let me list five factors.

First, it is true, the Resurrection narratives are different in the four Gospels. But the basic difference lies in the accounts of the appearances of Jesus to his disciples and friends, not in the accounts of how women (and others) found the tomb of Jesus empty.

Second, the Gospel writers clearly had *different* accounts of the appearances *in their sources.* But that is not odd because the post-Resurrection appearances would have been originally reported by the various apostles to encourage faith in the risen Christ. But different apostles would be likely to report different appearances on different occasions as they went round preaching and teaching. Acts 1:3 implies (and 1 Corinthians 15:5–7 proves) that there were many more appearances to the disciples than are recorded in the Gospels. So we would expect there to be different memories and traditions of the appearances.

Third, the Gospel writers clearly had *similar* accounts of the Empty Tomb *in their sources*. When we look at the narratives of the Empty Tomb we see a remarkable unanimity. The three Synoptic Gospels (Matthew, Mark and Luke) all agree on three things: one, that Mary Magdalene and some other women went to the tomb of Jesus on the first day of the week and found the stone rolled away from the tomb's entrance; two, that a young man (or some angelic presence) explained what had happened: 'He has risen, he is not here'; and, three, that the women were frightened and left the tomb.

Fourth, John 20:1–2 is very similar to the Synoptic outline:

> Now on the first day of the week Mary Magdalene came to the tomb early, while it was still dark, and saw that the stone had been taken away from the tomb. So she ran [? frightened], and went to Simon Peter and the other disciple, the one whom Jesus loved, and said to them, 'They have taken the Lord out of the tomb, and we [? Mary *and the other women*] do not know where they have laid him.'

The only difference in John is that the angelic interpreter has not been mentioned. But two angels are mentioned in verses 11–13 when Mary is back at the empty tomb.

Fifth, in their sources, the Gospel writers were drawing on different accounts that *agreed* over the Empty Tomb. And, remember, Mark's Gospel is generally reckoned to be written in the sixties of the first century. The information all the Gospel writers drew on was preached, remembered and (perhaps) recorded by others much earlier. But that takes us back right into the days of those who saw the risen Jesus. Even as late as A.D. 56 when Paul was writing 1 Corinthians he tells us that many of the disciples who had seen Jesus after the Resurrection 'are still alive, though some have fallen asleep' (15:6). It is unthinkable that any eye-witnesses would have allowed an Empty Tomb tradition to develop so uniformly if it was fiction.

The nature of the tradition

But what about the Bishop of Durham's second problem, the

nature of the tradition?

We are fortunate in having a first-hand account of the Resurrection tradition — it is the tradition Paul himself received and recorded in 1 Corinthians 15:3–8:

> For I delivered to you as of first importance what I also received, that Christ died for our sins in accordance with the scriptures, that he was buried, that he was raised on the third day in accordance with the scriptures, and that he appeared to Cephas, then to the twelve. Then he appeared to more than five hundred brethren at one time, most of whom are still alive, though some have fallen asleep. Then he appeared to James, then to all the apostles. Last of all, as to one untimely born, he appeared also to me.

Written earlier than the Gospels, this Epistle was written at most twenty-six years after the first Easter. But the tradition Paul had 'received' probably went back much earlier to his meeting with Peter in Jerusalem three years after his conversion (Gal 1:18). This discussion took place no more than four to eight years after the events recorded in 'the tradition'! Paul would have heard from those with first-hand experience the details of the death and Resurrection of Jesus.

Now Paul makes it quite clear in 1 Corinthians 15 that whatever differences there might be in the primitive faith and preaching, there was unanimity over certain fundamental elements of belief. There were, in fact, four fundamentals (or matters 'of first importance'). The fact that Christ died; the fact that he was buried; the fact that he was raised; and the fact that he appeared. What does this tell us?

First, the tradition focused on the burial in addition to the death of Christ. The Gospels show that Joseph of Arimathea was remembered by the Christians precisely because he played a prominent part in the burial. There was no doubt, therefore, about the tomb where Jesus had been put. And as F. F. Bruce says: 'Burial . . . emphasizes the reality of the resurrection which followed, as a divine act which reversed the act of men.'[6] It points to the Empty Tomb.

Second, the tradition made it clear that the Resurrection was an event 'on the third day'. But what could give rise to

this date? Had there been no Empty Tomb but only vision-
ary experiences, why should these be dated to 'the third
day'? 'He was raised' is a quite separate element in the tradition from 'he appeared'. The date is not when Christ
appeared but when he was raised. The only evidence of
dating we have is that of the discovery of the empty tomb on
the first day of the week, which was the third day after the
burial. This too points to the Empty Tomb.

Third, the tradition made it clear that the Resurrection
was not a statement about the nature of God, but it was
'according to the Scriptures'. God was *fulfilling* his promises
and bringing in the new age.

Fourth, the tradition made it clear that the Christians must
believe *both* 'that he was raised on the third day' *and* 'that he
appeared'. The appearances by themselves are not 'gospel'.
Some of the early disciples thought an appearance was just a
psychical experience (Lk 24:37). Nor is the discovery of the
empty tomb on the third day by itself 'gospel'. To Mary
Magdalene it suggested not Resurrection but removal of the
body. The Empty Tomb and the appearances *must* go together. They point to the *nature* of the Resurrection. The
Empty Tomb pointed to continuity with Christ's former
bodily existence. The appearances pointed to discontinuity
as well. Christ was not crudely resuscitated but God had
worked a supernatural act of transformation and re-creation.
He was no longer bound by time and space. In Paul's vocabulary it was, paradoxically, a body that was both cor-
poreal and spiritual! That is why there is ambiguity about the
descriptions of the seeing of the risen Jesus, including the
description of Paul's own experience in Acts.

Stories to support religious beliefs

It seems evident that Paul believed in the Empty Tomb and
the bodily Resurrection of Christ. The whole argument and
vocabulary of 1 Corinthians 15 presupposes bodily change
pattern on Christ's Resurrection ('We shall not all sleep,

but we shall all be changed' (v.51); 'Death is *swallowed up* in victory' (v.54); cf. 2 Cor 4:4, where in the Greek the Resurrection body is likened to an overcoat *put on over* other clothes, not *instead* of them). And his tradition is compatible with the speeches in Acts. There you have the Resurrection as the reversal of the burial in the tomb. Peter at Pentecost says: 'David . . . died and was buried, *and his tomb is with us to this day.'* But Christ's tomb, he implies, is not like David's, for 'his flesh' did not 'see corruption' (Acts 2:29,31). Paul himself says at Pisidian Antioch: 'they took him down from the tree, and laid him in a tomb. But God raised him from the dead' (Acts 13:29–30).

But what about the claim that stories are generated to support religious beliefs? Three things need to be said.

First, the Empty Tomb as a story by itself would prove nothing. The Jewish authorities thought it could mean the disciples had stolen the body. Nor would there have been a need to generate Empty Tomb stories. A spiritual Resurrection, if that is what it was, would have been easier to get people to accept than a bodily Resurrection. Jews only expected a bodily resurrection at 'the end'.

Second, if Jews were going to generate a story about an empty tomb, there is no way they would have made women the first to discover it. For Jews disregarded the evidence of women.

Third, we can, however, admit that early in the Christian proclamation the Empty Tomb may not have needed stressing, but the later proclamation possibly had to spell it out more in the face of spiritualizing and Gnosticizing tendencies. This, indeed, is an 'appropriate story to support religious belief'. But it is appropriate because it is true!

In conclusion, we have seen that none of the reasons appealed to by the Bishop of Durham should make him 'wholly uncertain about the Empty Tomb as literal historical fact.' The Empty Tomb, rather, should be believed as it coheres with the biblical account of the material world. Christ's Resurrection is one of the 'first-fruits'. Paul sees ultimately the creative power of God transforming the whole material universe: 'The creation itself will be set free from its bondage to decay and obtain the glorious liberty of the children of God' (Rom 8:21). True, the New Testament speaks of the discontinuity between the new and old order; but there are hints of continuity as well — the Empty Tomb being one of them!

John Polkinghorne, formerly Professor of Mathematical Physics at Cambridge, now ordained, writes: 'If one believes that the tomb was empty, as I do, certain consequences follow . . . [One] thing that the empty tomb says to me is that matter has a destiny, a transformed and transmuted destiny no doubt, but a destiny nevertheless. The material creation is not a transient, even mistaken episode. Of course that is a deeply mysterious thought.'[7]

6

The beginnings of subversion

If denial of the Virgin Birth and doubt over the Empty Tomb are contrary to Anglican tradition and hard to justify in terms of the evidence, how is it that we have bishops and theologians in the Church who are unbelieving in this respect?

Begin at the beginning — the Deists

It is difficult to know where to start the story. Some, no doubt, would suggest we start with the serpent in the Garden of Eden! Because there is so much talk about symbolism today, we could start with Hegel and his influence on David Strauss in the nineteenth century in Germany. But possibly a better point of departure is in the eighteenth century in England.

A former Bishop of Durham, Joseph Butler (1692–1752), made the following remark about those days:

> It is come, I know not how, to be taken for granted by many persons that Christianity is not so much as a subject of inquiry; but that it is now at length discovered to be fictitious. And accordingly they treat it as if, in the present age, this were an agreed point among all people of discernment; and nothing remained, but to set it up as a principal subject of mirth and ridicule, as it were by way of reprisals, for its having so long interrupted the pleasures of the world.[1]

No age is exactly like another; but there are some simi-

70

larities between the mid-twentieth century and the period Bishop Butler was referring to — the end of the seventeenth century and the first half of the eighteenth. It was a time of scientific confidence but social and religious confusion. Newton (1642–1727) in England had discovered the mathematics of planetary motion; Leibnitz (1646–1716) in Germany had developed the calculus; Huygens (1629–95) in Holland had developed the wave theory of light and invented the pendulum clock; Hobbes (1588–1679) had rocked the world with his views of social and political determinism. The Church was exhausted after the civil wars between 1642 and 1660 and many were wearied with wrangling over such things as signing with the sign of the cross in baptism, wearing surplices and kneeling to receive holy communion. Disillusionment had set in, as had decadence; for the world of Bishop Butler was a world of permissiveness; frank, explicit plays were the order of the day.

A year before Butler was born, Robert Boyle (1627–91), the 'father of chemistry', died. He had taken part in setting up the Royal Society in 1662. But in his will he decreed that money should be provided for eight sermons:

> For proving the Christian religion against notorious infidels, namely Atheists, *Theists*, Pagans, Jews and Mahometans, not descending lower to any controversies that are among Christians themselves.[2]

We can see from this that Boyle did not want Christians arguing over secondary matters; he wanted a sense of proportion. However, he was quite clear about one thing. You could believe in God, but still be 'an infidel'.

In Boyle's day there were people who believed in God (the God Christians spoke about) and so could be called theists, but they had to be opposed. Why? Because the Church at this time was engaged in a battle for survival. The enemy was what we today call Deism (Boyle called it Theism). We have already made reference to it.

One of the early Boyle lecturers was Samuel Clarke (1675–1729). He spoke of the Deists like this in 1704:

> They see that things generally go on in a constant and regular method; that the frame and order of the world are preserved by things being disposed and managed in an uniform manner; that certain causes produce certain effects in a continued succession, according to certain fixed laws or rules; and from hence they conclude, very weakly and unphilosophically, that there are in *matter* certain necessary *laws* or *powers,* the result of which is that which they call the *course of nature,* which they think is impossible to be changed or altered, and consequently that there can be no such thing as *miracles.*[3]

Clarke identified four types of Deist. At the risk of over-simplifying, a thumb-nail sketch of the beliefs of a Deist of the late seventeenth and eighteenth centuries would be something like this: he believed in God, but a God who didn't 'interfere' in the life of the world; he believed that Christianity was good for the English, but all religions actually lead to God; he believed in Jesus, but held that what he believed about him depended more on Reason than Revelation; he believed that 'nature' ruled supreme, therefore he did not believe in miracles and so he rejected the Virgin Birth and the Empty Tomb.

Thomas Woolston (1670–1733), for example, a Cambridge clergyman, argued that the New Testament miracles had to be interpreted allegorically or symbolically and as far as the Resurrection was concerned you had to give a 'mystical interpretation of the whole story'. John Toland (1670–1722) said Christianity was 'not mysterious'. Although he discredited the Canon, he said he stood by the Bible, but only as he interpreted it! He didn't deny revelation, he just emptied it of value. He only accepted revelation that fitted in with *his* reason, and suggested that the original simplicity of the gospel had been transformed under pagan influence. He refused to allow for there to be paradox in God's plan.

Bishop Butler

These ideas were, however, never accepted as part of the Church's teaching. Indeed both by legal action and by argument they were opposed.

There was some direct, if quaint, orthodox defending of the faith. Bishop Sherlock (1678–1761) replied to Woolston with a *Trial of the Witnesses*. It was an argument for the historic reality of the Resurrection. His conclusion was in the form of a legal verdict:

> JUDGE: What say you. Are the Apostles guilty of giving false evidence in the case of the resurrection of Jesus, or not guilty?
> FOREMAN OF THE JURY: Not guilty.

Before long these Deist ideas merged with Unitarian and Arian ideas. Like the Arians in the fourth century, people were denying the full deity of Christ. Even Richard Watson (1737–1816), a Professor of Divinity at Cambridge, later an absentee Bishop of Llandaff, and great-great-great grandfather of David Watson defended Unitarianism.

However, in spite of this spread of Deist ideas, one hundred years after the publication of Toland's *Christianity Not Mysterious* (1696) Edmund Burke could dismiss the Deists as a school of writers wholly ignored and largely forgotten. Why was that?

There were two factors. First, there were some remarkably able Christian apologists who entered the lists. These included Bishop Butler of Durham himself who published *The Analogy of Religion, Natural and Revealed, to the Constitution and Course of Nature* in 1736.

Butler argued that in practical matters you could only go on probabilities; but the sensible man had to commit himself to what was probable: *practical and factual matters don't admit of mathematical certainty*. Nor is there anything odd about this; it is the way things are in nature. By analogy it would not be unreasonable if that were the way things are in Scripture and revelation. We should not expect Scripture to be different to nature and the rest of life, including religious experience.

Butler liked the remark of Origen (the early theologian from Alexandria, c.185 254):

He, who believes the Scripture to have proceeded from him who is the author of nature, may well expect to find the same sort of difficulties in it as are found in the constitution of nature.

John Wesley

The second factor in the defence of the apostolic Christian faith was the spiritual revival under John Wesley (1703–91). Norman Sykes sums it up well:

> The Methodist revival turned the flank of the Deist and Arian controversies; for sinners convinced of the fact of sin and the reality of redemption, wasted no time in abstract theorizing about the precise definition of the Deity of Christ who had saved them. Perhaps this was the most important immediate influence of Wesley on the religion of his age. 'We are not to fight against notions, but against sins.' But in driving sins out of the door, a good many notions fled also out of the window.[4]

The story of Wesley's and Whitefield's evangelical preaching in Britain and America is well known. So is the occasion in 1739 when John Wesley met Bishop Butler in Bristol. Here were the two great defenders of the faith. But according to Wesley, Bishop Butler said during the course of the interview:

> I once thought you and Mr Whitefield well-meaning men; but I cannot think so now . . . Sir, the pretending to extraordinary revelations and gifts of the Holy Ghost is a horrid thing, a very horrid thing.

To this, however, Wesley replied that he was not responsible for Mr Whitefield, but that:

> I pretend to no extraordinary revelations or gifts of the Holy Ghost; none but what every Christian may receive, and ought to expect and pray for.[5]

Wesley actually read Butler's *Analogy* travelling between Alnwick and Morpeth in Northumberland: 'a fine book . . . but I doubt it is too hard for most of those it was chiefly intended.'[6]

Two of the greatest Anglicans of the time may not have seen eye to eye on everything, but it could be argued, that under God, they saved the Church of England.

Wesley, of course, had had that experience on May 24th 1738 in London. He wrote:

> In the evening I went very unwillingly to a society in Aldersgate Street, where one was reading Luther's preface to the *Epistle to the Romans.* About a quarter to nine, while he was describing the change which God works in the heart through faith in Christ, I felt my heart strangely warmed. I felt that I did trust in Christ, Christ alone, for salvation; and an assurance was given me that he had taken away my sins, even *mine,* and saved me from the law of sin and death.[7]

Wesley later preached in churches and in fields. Together with Whitefield, from whom he differed on some matters, he helped change the religious face of the nation. Whitefield was the great preacher and Wesley the great organizer. 'Wherever Whitefield went,' writes G. R. Cragg, 'he left an overwhelming impression of impassioned eloquence; wherever Wesley went he left a company of men and women closely knit together in a common life.'[8]

The followers of John Wesley and the Church of England later parted company over the question of ordination. But Wesley, to his dying day, considered himself quite rightly an ordained clergyman of the Church of England.

There was, however, far more to the Evangelical revival than the Methodist followers of John Wesley. *Anglican* Evangelicalism was where much of the strength of this spiritual revival lay.

Evangelicals

Evangelicals were committed to seeing people built up in the local church and seeing these churches grow. One of the early Evangelicals, Grimshaw (1708–63) of Haworth, West Yorkshire (later the home of the Brontë's), was questioned by the Archbishop of York in 1749 about the parish. He reported that when he went there he found twelve communicants. But now 'in winter, between three and four hundred, according to the weather. In summer sometimes nearer twelve hundred.'

W. W. Champneys (1807–75), an Evangelical of a later period, was appointed to Whitechapel in 1837. He found a completely empty church. In 1851 there were three services a Sunday, and on the day of the census, there were 1,547 present in the morning, 827 in the afternoon, and 1,643 in the evening. We tend to think that there was something inevitable about church-going in the nineteenth century and that there is something inevitable about people not going to church in the twentieth. But it needs to be remembered that many churches were empty in the eighteenth century. It was the Evangelicals and then the Tractarians that made England a church-going nation. There is, therefore, nothing *inevitable* about our current secularism.

One of the most distinguishing marks of the Evangelicals was that they took their Christianity seriously. They were people of the Bible. Speaking of Church people of his day William Wilberforce, the great Evangelical and the man who worked so hard for the abolition of the slave trade, said this:

> Their opinions on the subject of religion are not formed from the perusal of the Word of God. The Bible lies on the shelf unopened; and they would be wholly ignorant of its contents, except for what they hear occasionally at church, or for the faint traces which their memories may still retain of the lessons of their earliest infancy.[9]

They preached for men and women to be converted to Jesus Christ in a personal way, but they were against a wrong sort of emotionalism. 'Don't tell me of your feelings,' John Newton is reported to have said; 'a traveller would be glad of fine weather, but, if he be a man of business, he will go on.'

The Evangelicals supported missionary work and indeed they were responsible for the great modern worldwide missionary movement.

The Evangelicals had a political orientation, too. They

believed that the State had a God-given function, and so it should be made aware of its duties, and that was the Church's job. If this involved political conflict, as was the case with Wilberforce and the abolition of slavery, so be it. The *Christian Observer,* the first of the Evangelical journals, wasn't afraid of current 'hot' political issues. Note these words written in 1832:

> We pity the heart and the head of any man, especially a clergyman, who, when addressed upon the duty he owes to God and his country in regard to such momentous topics as Ecclesiastical Reform [and] the abolition of the anti-Christian system of West-Indian slavery . . . can affect to stigmatize such considerations under the absurd name of 'politics', wrapping himself up in his own little selfish circle.[10]

Evangelical influence on the Church and nation in the nineteenth century was enormous. Charles Simeon (1759–1836), perhaps the greatest of all the Evangelicals, spent his life at Holy Trinity, Cambridge. Because of the undergraduates, fellows, masters of colleges and others who sat under his long ministry, he exercised far more influence on the Church and the world than any bishop or archbishop. Many who had been helped and instructed by Simeon went on to hold responsible positions in Britain and abroad.

By the end of the nineteenth century, 50 per cent of the Church of England was, at grass-roots level, Evangelical. Parishes supporting the Church Missionary Society then numbered 5,700 — nearly half the churches in the land (and the C.M.S. was the Evangelicals' missionary society).

But the Evangelical cause waned. Why was that?

Modernism

Many reasons can be given as to why Evangelicalism weakened at the end of the nineteenth century. One reason might have been that second generation Evangelicals wasted their energies fighting with second generation Tractarians over some secondary matters in the Ritualist controversies. Be that as it may, it was at this point that the subversion of the Church of England began in earnest the phenomenon called Modernism.

Writing in 1927, J. F. Bethune-Baker, Professor of Divinity at Cambridge, himself a leading Modernist, explained the history of the movement:

> Though the modernism we have to deal with is an ecclesiastical and theological phenomenon of the last thirty years only, its roots go much further back. They go back in the sphere of biblical criticism *at least as far as the English Deists of the eighteenth century* [italics mine], whose influence passed through Bolingbroke and his friendship with Voltaire to France, and on to Germany — coming back to England, all the stronger for being a little humanized, in the middle of the last century.[11]

Modernism was Deism in modern dress!

The history of the Modernist movement in the Church of England has now been excellently surveyed by Alan Stephenson in *The Rise and Decline of English Modernism,* which is essential reading for understanding the predicament of the Church of England in the 1980s.

A full account of the development of the movement in England would have to take account of the work *Essays and Reviews* published in 1860. Already in Germany, Strauss had published in 1835 his *Leben Jesu.* George Eliot translated it into English in 1846; and the faithful of the Church of England were then able to read that the Virgin Birth and the Resurrection need not be regarded as historically true. Now those same faithful were having clergy of their own Church cast doubt on the Bible — or so it seemed. In fact from 1860 onwards the Church was subjected to a barrage of questions.

However, there are reasons why the views of the Modernists, as they soon came to be called, gained the currency they did. First, there was a default by Evangelicals to engage in serious theological scholarship and to be willing to face issues. This wasn't made good until the end of the Second World War and the renaissance of Evangelical scholarship that has been occurring since then in both the United Kingdom and the United States.

Secondly, while the Evangelicals were escaping from difficult questions into various forms of biblical obscurantism, their Tractarian brethren were escaping into various forms of ritualistic romanticism. Then they fought each other! The accounts of these ritualistic controversies do not make pleasant reading. No doubt serious doctrinal issues were at stake, but a vacuum was being created which was being filled by a faction that was denying the Virgin Birth and the Empty Tomb.

The third reason why Modernism in the Church of England was so successful, was that it had all the ingredients necessary for it to become a movement. It had a leader, a strategy, a conference, a theological college and a journal. The leader was an able clergyman by the name of Henry Major; the strategy was to get influence at Oxford and Cambridge; the conferences were regular and became major events from the Girton Conference in Cambridge (1921) to the Somerville Conference in Oxford (1967). (It was this last conference that effectively signalled the end of the Modernist movement in the Church of England.) The theological college was Ripon Hall, first at Ripon, then at Oxford (now merged with another college); the journal was the *Modern Churchman* (still being published). This 'package' between the two World Wars meant that 'the Modern Churchmen's Union' exercised, indirectly, enormous influence.

Modernist beliefs

Alan Stephenson gives us a portrait of the typical English Modernist:

> He was totally convinced of the existence of God . . . but a god who worked only through the evolutionary process . . . He believed in a God who could be known, to a certain extent, in other religions, but who was supremely revealed in the Logos. He had no doubt about the existence of Jesus Christ, though he was prepared to admit that if it were proved that Jesus had never existed, that would not mean the end of his religious faith. His Christology was a degree Christology and adoptionist. His Jesus was . . . 'the Lord of Thought' who proclaimed the Fatherhood of God and the Brotherhood of Man. His doctrine of the Atone-

ment was Abelardian and exemplarist. He had no hesitation in accepting all that biblical criticism had to say, as far as it had advanced by the death of B. H. Streeter in 1937. He maintained that he believed in the supernatural, but *not in the miraculous. His Jesus, therefore, did not perform miracles. He was not born of a Virgin and his resurrection was a spiritual one. The tomb was not empty.*[12]

But men openly holding these views were *not* made bishops.

In essence the Modernist was, and is, a 'revisionist'. The conclusion of his thinking was, according to Bethune-Baker:

That all theological formulas must be tested by their correspondence with religious experience, that their values are not speculative but practical . . . we should concentrate our attention on *the religious construction* of all our traditional doctrines: that we should be regarded as pledged, when we affirm them, not to belief in the intellectual propositions they plainly set before us, or the particular happenings or facts of history which they assert or imply, but to the values or meanings for conduct and the attitude to life which those particular beliefs conveyed or expressed for the men of old who had them.[13]

This is an interesting proposal, but it seems to have little to do with the faith of the Church of England as we have seen it to be or with the faith of the apostolic Church! What we have here is a 'vague faith' in a 'vague Christ'. The only facts are:

The religious experience of Jesus Himself and the religious experience of others of which He was at once the immediate cause and the centre. It is the substance of the Faith thus originated that matters, and the doctrinal system of the Church is of value as preserving and mediating and stimulating that Faith in all varieties of historical surroundings, so that its formulations must be elastic and adaptable to the ever-changing historical surroundings.[14]

This is what we seem to be hearing from a number of bishops in the Church of England. It is an attempt to make the Christian faith independent of the conclusions of biblical research and thus history. But it can't be done: if Christ is not risen (the Resurrection fact), our faith (the Resurrection faith) is in vain!

7

Modernism and the Bible

The liberal Modernist Movement came from the enthusiastic study of the origins of the Church and its early literature. Much of this work was carried on in Germany in the nineteenth century. The starting point for the work was that the Bible had to be studied like any other book of ancient literature and history. This was the position of Benjamin Jowett in *Essays and Reviews* that had caused such a storm in 1860. In his essay 'On the interpretation of Scripture' he had urged people 'to read Scripture like any other book'.

The term *Modernism* is a term that has gone out of use. This may be because in 1967 at the Somerville Conference, Modernism in one sense came to an end in the Church of England. It may also be because Modernists don't use the term of themselves any longer, as they wrongly think that *everybody* now shares their liberal assumptions.

Liberal is an unfortunate word. It must not be taken as implying liberal political views when being used in theological discussion (in the same way, *conservative* must not be taken as implying conservative political views). It is also very much a relative concept. It means *more* liberal than some other (accepted) positions. So as much as possible we should try to use the terms *Modernism* and *Modernist* as shorthand for the views and attitudes of modern liberal theology.

The findings, as the Modernist saw them, of biblical criticism

were twofold. On the one hand he held that the first three
Gospels had all been composed quite a time after the events
they were describing. On the other hand these compositions
were 'coloured' by the interests and beliefs of the writers
(or churches) of this later period; and if this was true of the
first three Gospels, it was certainly true of the fourth Gospel.
This lead him to the conclusion that we can never really
know the historical Jesus; nothing, indeed, is certain about
him.

This position was spelt out by the Oxford New Testament
Professor, R. H. Lightfoot (1883–1953) in 1935. His statement has now gained a certain notoriety:

> The form of the earthly no less than of the heavenly Christ is for
> the most part hidden from us. For all the inestimable value of the
> Gospels, they yield little more than a whisper of his voice; we
> trace in them but the outskirts of his ways.[1]

Lightfoot had a very great influence on a group of younger
New Testament scholars, who themselves have greatly influenced the Church of England. But these scholars have never
really answered the question 'How do you believe anything if
all is uncertain?'

Roman Catholics and Modernism

Alfred Loisy (1857–1940) was a French Roman Catholic
Modernist who suggested that you have to develop a theory
that the Christian faith can be independent of any of the
results of the historical and literary criticism of the Gospels.
Many have tried to follow that path since; indeed, this is the
focus of the current debate in the Church of England. It is
the position of some of the bishops. But the task is impossible, unless you want to stray into Gnosticism — for it was
Gnosticism that tried to drive a wedge between faith and
history in the early Church. But in the gruelling battle over
this issue in the early centuries, the Church gave a resound-
ing 'No!' to these Gnostic views. 'Such a separation of faith
from history is incompatible with a living faith in Jesus

Christ' was the clear message of the early Church. But the Modernist, committed as he is to biblical scepticism, has no other alternative.

Yet the Modernist wants to stay in the Church. He justifies this, according to Bethune-Baker, in the following way:

> The Christian revelation is not the revelation of a number of intellectual truths or propositions of a rational kind, but is the revelation of a way of life, an attitude to life and all its interests and activities, and therefore is social. It holds that this revelation is only to be understood and realised in a society with an ordered life of its own. And further, because it is convinced that in the historical society of the Church, whatever its formulas, there has always been true Christian experience, it cannot contemplate any severance from that stream of life. The synthesis it aims at must be effected in the Church itself.[2]

The ethics and social teaching of the gospel, however, depend on the historical facts of the gospel. Here lies the power of Christianity. This the Modernist fails to see. This is why Modernism is so dangerous. It destroys the historical basis of the Church but still wants to be in the fold, thus gaining credibility for its position. It doesn't seem to see that if the walls of the sheepfold are dismantled stone by stone, one day there will be no fold to be inside!

The Roman Catholic Church recognized this, however. It saw too that Modernist solutions to the problems posed by biblical scholarship simply would not do. However, it became somewhat heavy-handed, not distinguishing genuine problems from bad answers. Still, Pius X, it was said, 'was more interested in protecting the faithful than in the niceties of scientific attitude.' So, one after another of the Modernist books was condemned by the Roman authorities. A papal decree on July 3rd 1907, *Lamentabili sane exitu* and a papal encyclical on September 7th 1907, *Pascendi dominici gregis* outlawed Modernism from the Roman Church.

But it is one thing to reject bad answers; it is another thing to solve biblical problems. That was not done in the Roman Church. It decided to wait for Pius XII and his encyclical

Divino Afflante Spiritu in 1943. This gave more freedom to Roman scholars. It meant that the problems (and some suggested solutions) emerged again by the time of the Second Vatican Council.

The reliability of Scripture

In all of this we are seeing a 'battle for the Bible'. More correctly, it should be called a 'battle for the apostolic faith' (the Bible being the book where you discover the apostles' teaching).

The key issue is reliability. Does the Bible allow us, or does it not allow us to say anything definite about Jesus Christ? Or are all the Modernist views about the Bible correct? If we follow some recent presentations in the media and the suggestions of some 'doubting bishops', we might assume we have to give a negative verdict on the Bible.

But current thinking in many quarters indicates the contrary. We *can* be very positive about the life of Jesus as we look at the biblical evidence. The scepticism of the Modernists is unwarranted. There are three reasons why.

First, it is now seen that the alleged gap between the Gospel narratives and the events they describe is not so long after all. Mark's Gospel, it is usually agreed, was written at the most thirty-five years after the death and Resurrection of Jesus. That is less than the space between the present time and the end of the Second World War.

It was the New Testament scholar C. H. Dodd who said in the heady days of Modernism that he felt this gap to be a 'very serious matter'. But in later life he realized that this wasn't so at all. In a BBC radio programme in 1949 he said that he still had a very vivid memory of events of the summer of 1914 just prior to the outbreak of the First World War. So he said:

> When Mark was writing there must have been many people who were in their prime under Pontius Pilate, and they must have remembered the stirring and tragic events of that time at least as

vividly as we remember 1914. If anyone had tried to put over an entirely imaginary or fictitious account of them, there would have been middle-aged or elderly people who would have said (as you or I might say) 'you are wasting your breath: I remember it as if it were yesterday.'[3]

Second, there is a growing awareness that all our scientific knowledge about how the Gospels came to be constructed tells us little, one way or the other, about the truth or otherwise of what is reported. By itself it is not a reason for doubting as used to be thought. It may well be that the Gospels are the result of Christians in the mid-first century AD collecting earlier written sources and putting them into shape. This is what the Source Critics tell us. Or there may be something in what the Form Critics tell us, when they say the Gospels resulted in part from regularly told short stories about the life and teaching of Jesus. The suggestion of Redaction Criticism also seems reasonable that the material (from whatever source) was so put together that a particular theological truth is emphasized.

But none of this tells us whether what we have as the final product is a true and reliable picture of what happened or not. Scholars may say that this or that part of the Gospel narrative comes from 'Q' (a collection of Jesus' teachings) or from 'M' (Matthew's special source) or that it comes in the 'form of a miracle story'. But that tells us absolutely nothing about whether *what* comes in such a way is true or false. A miracle may be reported in a way that appears stylized, but that doesn't tell us much, for we want to know whether there was a miracle in the first place. Accounts of *how* the report of the miracle was transmitted do not necessarily answer that question.

Presupposition

Third, there is also a growing awareness of the nature of presupposition in New Testament scholarship. Indeed, there is a sharp reaction to New Testament scholars like Professor

Nineham (who, we have already mentioned, was the preacher at the Consecration of the new Bishop of Durham). His view is summed up in his own words like this:

> Since the historian's essential criteria presuppose the absence of radical abnormality or discontinuity, only those events can be described as 'historical' which are fully and exclusively human and entirely confined within the limits of this world.[4]

Such a view would be agreeable to Samuel Clarke's Deist! But the flaws are obvious. For as R. T. France puts it:

> The miraculous, and indeed all that transcends our normal materialistic categories of thought [now], falls outside the historian's proper sphere of reference and therefore cannot be called 'historical'. It is thus decreed in advance that the 'historical' Jesus, both in his deeds and in his words, will be compatible with the anti-supernaturalistic world-view (the closed mind) of modern scientific man . . . So it happens that whatever in the life or teaching of Jesus is incompatible with such a world-view *must* be pronounced unhistorical, or unauthentic, in the sense that it is the product of pious reflection and imagination, not of sober fact.[5]

Put another way, if you come to the Bible as so many have done with this presupposition, then obviously you have to rule out large parts of it as the product of the pious imagination of the early Church (the Virgin Birth and the Empty Tomb included) and call them symbols. Simply to state this approach is to demonstrate its folly. In the words of Frederick Temple at the time of *Essays and Reviews:* 'If the conclusions are prescribed, the study is precluded.'

Sub-Christian scholarship

It is right to look at the Bible as we look at other ancient texts. But that has to be qualified. For we have to ask at the same time what are our assumptions? What lenses do we have on when we look at it? For there is no such thing as 'plain glass'. Let me explain.

We can look at the Bible from a Christian perspective, or

we can look at it from a secularist perspective (or from all sorts of other perspectives). Quite often this makes no difference, but sometimes fundamental assumptions and beliefs are of critical importance. This is often the case when explanations of the biblical narrative have to be given. It could be a miracle story, for example, that has to be explained. For a miracle to be a miracle there has to be some degree of extraordinariness about it, and that requires some account or explanation. But what *counts* as a good explanation depends on your fundamental assumptions and beliefs.

The point is this: your world-view and your beliefs *as you look at the texts* are all important. If you cannot believe in a God who intervenes and who is a God of the miraculous, an explanation in terms of God's direct action in miracles will never satisfy you. Or if you tend to have a world-view that is dualistic — that regards matter as separate from spirit — you may find it hard to believe, for example, in the Virgin Birth or in the *bodily* Resurrection. You will find it hard in the case of other miracles to accept explanations that show God directly involved in nature. But if you accept the biblical evaluation of matter, if you see Jesus Christ as the pre-existent Lord now come in the flesh, *God incarnate,* you will be open to different possibilities and, therefore, explanations.

Basil Willey has written well on explanations:

> The clarity of an explanation seems to depend upon the degree of satisfaction that it affords . . . 'Explanation' may perhaps be roughly defined as a restatement of something in terms of the current interests and assumptions . . . All depends upon our presuppositions, which in turn depend upon our training, whereby we have come to regard (or to feel) one set of terms as ultimate, the other not.[6]

There is therefore a relativity to all explanations.

This is what is meant by saying there is a *Christian* and a *sub-Christian* approach to the historical and literary criticism of the Gospels. There is a Christian way of explaining and a sub-Christian way of explaining. The Christian way has Christian presuppositions — those given by the apostles (and so found in the Scriptures themselves) and witnessed to by the Church down the centuries; the sub-Christian way has presuppositions that are *other* than those of the apostles and the Church. Both can be scientific; both have to be free to ask radical questions. But the answers they give will often be different when called to provide explanations. In one sense to be a Christian is to have opted (for various *reasons*) for the Christian frame of reference or Christian explanatory system. Precisely why a person does so is given in their personal testimony.

No explanation is absolute. It is related to the presuppositions of those involved. People with one set of beliefs will find one type of explanation convincing. People with another set of beliefs will find a different type of explanation convincing.

Background beliefs

All this is so important because much of the teaching in some of our theological faculties and colleges is based on sub-Christian scholarship. And that is why we have theological confusion in the Protestant denominations (including the Church of England) today.

We have to see the rise of the Modernist movement against the background of nineteenth-century humanism and progressive evolutionary optimism. As Bethune-Baker said: 'It is fundamentally conditioned by recognition of the evolutionary process of the world and human history and that God is "in" the process.'[7]

Of course, evolutionary theory as a scientific suggestion as to how species have developed by variation and natural selection has to be judged on its own merits. Many (not all) judge it to be the best theory available. But by itself that does not allow us to create a whole philosophy of life out of it and say this is reality, and *believe* in Evolution with a capital E. Yet many Modernists have virtually done just this. The folly of doing so and then saying that the whole universe is on the *up* is seen when you switch from anthropology to cosmology. You then discover a theory that gives you, in the second law of thermodynamics, a 'running *down*' universe! The issues were well spelt out by Stephen Toulmin in an important essay entitled 'Contemporary Scientific Mythology' in 1957.[8]

All this is precisely what happened in the last century. Evolutionary optimism, with a belief in natural law, formed the background beliefs of liberal Protestantism. It was the German theologian, Karl Barth (1886–1968), who was the first major scholar to throw overboard these assumptions publicly. He personally rejected liberal Protestantism, not when he had another look at the texts, but when the First World War was about to break out around him. When all the important names of German theology were backing the Kaiser's war policies, he had a radical transformation. He wrote:

> Disillusioned by their conduct, I perceived that I should not be able any longer to accept their ethics and dogmatics, their biblical exegesis, their interpretation of history; that at least for me the theology of the nineteenth century had no future.[9]

Brainwashing

One important corollary of all we have been saying is this: if a person frequently accepts certain explanations as explanatory *when they are based on sub-Christian assumptions or beliefs,* his own assumptions and beliefs in time will be affected. This will happen either by reinforcing scepticism or by causing a person to lose belief and become sceptical. This latter situation is not uncommon. There are sad instances of young and enthusiastic Christians being called to the ministry, going to a college or university and there being subjected to modernistic theories about the origins of Christianity and the biblical documents and in consequence losing their faith. It is a sophisticated form of brainwashing!

It is not that such a person is convinced by the logic of reasoning. It is more that he is forced, because of lack of expertise, time and information, to accept the range of sub-Christian explanations to the problems of biblical exegesis and Christian origins that are common currency. He then inevitably, if only gradually, thinks in those categories. This in time changes his background beliefs and assumptions.

The power of a belief system is extremely strong. And what many of its proponents have failed to see is that liberal Protestant theology forms such a belief system. It forms a network or web of interconnecting theories, explanations, doctrines and assumptions just as much as the more traditional theologies have done over the centuries. Nor is there anything odd about this. But it has to be acknowledged. Such a network of beliefs, however, will not necessarily last for ever!

Indeed, the history of human science is the story of how huge edifices of explanatory systems have been replaced, one after the other. This was Basil of Cappadocia's thesis. It is most evident in the physical sciences. Ptolemy and his explanations were replaced by Copernicus and his. These completely changed the way the explanatory process worked with regard to astronomy. But it also happens in theology. This is precisely what happened with the Modernist movement. Liberal Protestantism provided a completely new explanatory process, replacing old fundamentalisms. But the Roman Catholic Church, as we have seen, said that this new explanatory process didn't work. The Church of England, corporately, sooner rather than later, will have to reach the same decision, but, at the same time, it mustn't stifle the search for *better* explanations.

Dual authorship

This problem of how we address ourselves to the biblical texts can be put in a different way. Traditionally in the Church the Bible has been seen to have dual authorship. On the one hand, as the Creed affirms, *God* 'has spoken through the prophets'; on the other hand it is *prophets* (and apostles) that have spoken God's word. As they were speaking, God spoke through them.

Perhaps insufficient weight had been paid to the personalities of these human agents of God's word. So in the nineteenth century, it was said that there was a need to look at the Bible as you look at any other book, for it is not a set of propositions out of heaven. It is God's word through historical narrative, poetry, wise sayings, prophetic oracles, Gospels, letters and visions. There is rich variety of style. *But* — and this must not be forgotten — if the Bible is also at the same time *God's* word through these various writings, you can't read the Bible *exactly* as you read any other book.

For if it is God's word to man, it is God's word to me (whether I am an archbishop, bishop, archdeacon, dean, canon, parish clergyman or lay person).

We can fail to realize this. Helmut Thielicke, the German theologian, calls it 'increasingly thinking in the third person rather than in the second person'. And he says:

> This transition from one to the other level of thought, from a personal relationship with God to a merely technical reference, usually is exactly synchronised with the moment that I no longer can read the word of Holy Scripture as a word to me, but only as the object of exegetical endeavours.[10]

That is why the fundamental divide in theology is so often not at the point of the precise exegesis of this verse or that verse of Scripture, or over the question of how accurate some descriptive narrative is, but it is the divide between those who believe that God actually does speak to men through the Bible, and those who don't. It is between those who have an attitude of openness to the Bible and those who haven't. Or more precisely, it is between those who prove their belief (that God speaks in this way) by approaching *with humility* the teaching of the prophets and apostles and those who don't. These humble believers go to the Bible to *learn* from God. After all, it was Jesus himself who said: 'Father, . . . thou hast hidden these things from the wise and understanding and revealed them to babes [i.e. the open-hearted]' (Mt 11:25).

Let Charles Simeon of Holy Trinity, Cambridge, the great Evangelical leader at the turn of the nineteenth century, tell us how he tried to do this. He writes, speaking of himself:

> The author feels it impossible to avow too distinctly that it is an invariable rule with him to endeavour to give to every portion of the Word of God its full and proper force, without considering what scheme it favours, or whose system it is likely to advance . . . Where the inspired writers speak in unqualified terms, he thinks himself at liberty to do the same; judging that they needed no instruction from *him* how to propagate the truth. *He is content to sit as a learner at the feet of the holy Apostles, and has no ambition to teach them how they ought to have spoken.*[11]

8

The beginnings of conversion

In his sermon at the Consecration of the Bishop of Durham in York Minster, Professor Dennis Nineham said this to the new Bishop and assembled congregation:

> Using the analytical tools with which our culture has been built, we can often see that statements in the Bible or the creeds which are historical in form, and were taken at their face value by our forefathers, in fact convey religious rather than historical truth.[1]

We have now seen the history behind this remark, and we have seen how sceptical is Professor Nineham's approach to the Bible. Professor Anthony Hanson has coined a phrase for this approach: 'the Nineham treatment'. He says: 'The Nineham treatment will discredit the historical reliability of *any* document.'[2] Hanson argues that this makes a nonsense of history.

Confusion and enlightenment

Unfortunately, many of us during the twentieth century have got immune to what the theologians and biblical scholars have been saying over the years, or rather we have almost been hypnotized by Modernism or liberal Protestantism. One man who saw the issues was R. C. Zaehner, the Spalding Professor of Eastern Religions and Ethics at Oxford. Writing about modern liberal Protestants, he refers to —

— the dear theologians, whose quantitative output continues to be prodigious but whom nobody ever reads except theology students (they have to) and the theologians themselves, who have to keep abreast of the latest theological fashion because that, apparently, is what they are paid to do.

He then refers to the irrelevance of what they are saying to the questions people actually ask:

'The dog barks but the caravan passes on', as a Turkish proverb says. The day of theology was already over in the eighteenth century except, of course, among the Germans who, as Charles Péguy rightly pointed out, 'delight in confusion. That is what they call depth'.[3]

Zaehner, of course, exaggerates. But he has a point. The eighteenth century brought about the end of much *Christian* theology in the nineteenth century. There was a 'sell-out' to the Enlightenment and what was the result? *Sub-Christian* theology!

But what was the Enlightenment? It is the name we usually give to the overall movement of thought that spread throughout Europe from the middle of the eighteenth century onwards. It was related, therefore, to Deism and subsequently Modernism. But simply speaking, it was the result of the advance of science we earlier referred to. There was a feeling that the world had at last become 'enlightened'. Light had dawned and man had come of age.

In 1759 the French mathematician D'Alembert wrote about this:

The discovery and application of a new method of philosophising, the kind of enthusiasm which accompanies discoveries, a certain exaltation of ideas which the spectacle of the universe produces in us — all these courses have brought about a lively fermentation of minds. Spreading through nature in all directions like a river which has burst its dams, this fermentation has swept with a sort of violence everything along with it which stood in its way.[4]

The fundamental belief was in the absolute priority of

natural law. Nature ruled supreme and was simply waiting to have her secrets unlocked by science. And these secrets would be in the form of natural laws. 'Nature and nature's laws lay hid in night. God said: "Let Newton be", and all was light,' to quote Alexander Pope.

The net result was a 'closed' universe. 'God, if he exists, is the God of the Deists or a non-interventionist God,' or so people said: 'he set the whole show going. It now has to run according to the rules. The miraculous obviously can't happen.'

There was great confidence in the power of science. So *methods* appropriate for solving the problems of machines, mathematics and physics were automatically assumed appropriate for solving the problems of man, history and religion. Too few asked the basic question: 'Is man a machine?'

Lessing

A leading figure of the 'Enlightenment generation' was the German theologian and dramatist Gotthold Lessing (1729–81). His influence has been enormous, and in a sense he began the Modernist movement in theology.

He influenced *Essays and Reviews*. For example, the first and ill-fated article (because it later had to be withdrawn) by Frederick Temple was entitled *The Education of the World*. This was probably inspired by Temple's reading of Lessing's *The Education of the Human Race*. And it was Lessing who taught that you must 'interpret the Bible like any other book' — the theme of Benjamin Jowett's essay in *Essays and Reviews*.

Lessing's most famous piece of writing was a short essay *On the Proof of the Spirit and of Power*.[5] His argument went something like this: If I had seen Christ do miracles, I would have believed in him on that basis. If today there were still miracles happening, what could prevent me from accepting this proof of the spirit and of power, as the apostle calls it?

But I do not experience miracles. All I have to go on is the reports of others. But these reports are

> only . . . as reliable as historical truths ever can be. And then it is added that historical truths cannot be demonstrated [i.e. proved like the truths of mathematics]: nevertheless we must believe them as firmly as truths that have been demonstrated . . . If no historical truth can be demonstrated, then nothing can be demonstrated by means of historical truths. That is: *accidental truths of history can never become the proof of necessary truths of reason.*

As Professor Henry Chadwick has said: 'It may be doubted whether any writing equally influential in the history of modern religious thought has been marked by a comparable quantity of logical ambiguity.'[6] That is another way of saying he is confusing or, more likely, confused!

Lessing seems to be distinguishing 'accidental truths of history' (past events that happened) from 'necessary truths of reason' (the truths of mathematics or the truth of a syllogism in logic; here the truth *necessarily* comes from the ideas or meanings of the words). So he seems to be saying that the truth about the past can never be established by a 'proof' such as we can have in mathematics or logic. Who would want to disagree? That is obviously so. But the implied conclusion that has undermined the faith (or the potential faith) of millions, a conclusion still advocated by Modernist archbishops, bishops, clergy and laity, is this: 'We, therefore, can't be certain about the past and we can't "prove" that things in the past happened.' And that is totally false.

Of course, certainty comes from proof. With regard to something in the past, it is reasonable to want to prove that it happened. But to assume that there is *only one way of proving* — as in mathematics or a syllogism — is sheer nonsense. Mathematics (or logic) is one thing. History is another. And so are the physical sciences. What we have to do is prove things in ways that are *appropriate* to whatever it is we are trying to prove. Proof, for example, in the physical sciences can be quite unlike 'logical' proof, for it often occurs when an experiment works in specified conditions. Proof in a court of law is different again. Here, indeed, we are dealing with the 'accidental truths of history'. But the courts have their agreed procedures for establishing or proving the truth.

Faith and commitment

But Lessing went one stage further. He suggested it was unreasonable to make *commitments* on the basis of historical facts. He was so bewitched by 'pure reason' (logical, mathematical reasoning).

Let me quote him again:

> We all believe that an Alexander lived who in a short time conquered almost all Asia. But who, on the basis of this belief, would risk anything of great, permanent worth, the loss of which would be irreparable? . . . Certainly not I. Now I have no objection to raise against Alexander and his victory; but it might still be possible that the story was founded on a mere poem of Choerilus [here we have the 'Nineham treatment' in embryo].

There is, of course, not much doubt about Alexander. But as the historicity of Alexander is, usually, of little importance, we would not want to take a risk on it. However, the historicity of Jesus Christ *will be of supreme importance if he is God incarnate!* His historicity then matters, and some risks may have to be taken.

This was Bishop Butler's contention. His view was that in practical affairs we have to make commitments on probabilities. I commit myself to a train at King's Cross after all the evidence points to the fact that it is the Newcastle train. My certainty is *sufficient*. It is not watertight in the sense that the conclusion of a syllogism is watertight. But I can't for ever be making sure, otherwise I will miss my train. I can't forever be asking questions of the booking-clerk or the station-master. I can't forever be checking if they are sure there hasn't been some change of plan or if they are sure they are not suffering from amnesia! I will never be certain in the same way as I am certain of a proposition in mathematics.

But in practical affairs you make commitments on *sufficient* certainty.

So it is with the Virgin Birth and the Empty Tomb. The evidence is sufficient. It is not watertight — nor could it ever be in a mathematical sense. But we *can't forever be asking questions*. We have to make a commitment on sufficient certainty. And, as with the train, confirmation (or further proof) occurs on the journey (or life of faith). We know we are going in the right direction by what we subsequently see and experience.

The power of Lessing's attitude, however, has been enormous. It has ridden on the back of Enlightenment or Modernist attitudes. It superficially is claiming to be scientific — as though doubt in itself is more scientific than belief. For enlightenment, man thought that knowledge came through questioning all received opinions. This is fair enough, until doubt is made a virtue. To continue being sceptical when the reasonable thing is to believe is not clever but stupid.

However, such was the magic of the (unacknowledged) belief in sceptical reason that for some it almost became impossible to believe anything in the aftermath of the Enlightenment! Over the past 200 years in the West we have seen an increasing 'privatization' of beliefs. You have to be very tentative about them and have to apologize for them; you cannot bring them into the public sphere, because they are not strong enough! This is the result of the Enlightenment and some of the quite unfounded assumptions then made. Michael Polanyi sums it up like this:

> Belief was so thoroughly discredited that, apart from specially privileged opportunities . . . modern man lost his capacity to accept any explicit statement as his own belief. All belief was reduced to the status of subjectivity.[7]

All change

But things are changing. Perhaps 1984 will be remembered

not for David Watson, David Jenkins or Billy Graham, but for Bishop Lesslie Newbigin (a former bishop in the Church of South India). He wrote a brilliant little book for the British Council of Churches called *The other side of 1984*. The World Council of Churches then saw fit to publish it and give it a wider audience. Clifford Longley of *The Times* described it as 'one of the very few theological monographs of the past 10 years which is worth reading twice' (March 26th 1982). In it he reminds us of the force of Polanyi's arguments as he works out his own argument.

Lesslie Newbigin summarizes his position like this:

> I have started from the perception, which I believe to be valid and widely shared, that we are nearing the end of the period of 250 years during which our modern European culture has been confidently offering itself to the rest of the world as the torch-bearer for human progress. Following Polanyi, I have suggested that we are in a situation which has significant analogies with that which St. Augustine faced [i.e. at the break up of the Greco-Roman civilisation]. A uniquely brilliant culture was coming to the end of its life. It had lost the power to renew itself. What Augustine offered was nothing based upon the 'self-evident' axioms of classical culture. It was a new model, a new framework for understanding and coping with experience, based upon the fact that God had become incarnate in the man Jesus and had thereby manifested and put into effect God's purpose for all history and for every human soul.[8]

Newbigin, surely, is right. We have undoubtedly come to the end of the scientific world-view, though not, I hasten to add, to the end of science when treated humbly and properly.

Ironically, outside theological circles, in philosophy and science, radical changes in understanding have been taking place. Let us discuss these further.

In the nineteenth century, a scientific theory would quite often have been considered a *real picture* of the world. Things *really* were like the theory. But developments this century meant that, in physics especially, scientific theories were seen to be not quite so straightforward after all. It was becoming more and more difficult to make quantum theory into a representation or picture of reality. There were problems over the wave-particle duality in the theory of light. Heisenberg's uncertainty principle is the problem at its most acute. If you know where an electron is, you cannot know what it is doing. If you know what it is doing, you cannot know where it is!

In the wake of all this the philosophers got to work. They were aware that the public were being hoodwinked by some of the scientific popularizers. The great Sir James Jeans tried to explain the General Theory of Relativity by asking people to picture the universe as the three-dimensional surface of a four-dimensional balloon. No wonder Jeans could call the universe 'mysterious'. As was so clearly pointed out, he was making nonsense of language. A surface can, by definition, only refer to what is two-dimensional. People were being asked to visualize self-contradictions. Similarly a wave is a continuous flow and a particle is logically something very different.

So the philosophers of science were saying that, certainly in physics, theories were not so much descriptions of reality as 'models'; and they spoke of 'inferring techniques'. The august 'laws of nature' were being reduced to the 'laws of our methods of picturing things'.

Some, no doubt, overreacted to the old scientific orthodoxies. The debate, therefore, has continued. But these philosophical considerations have meant that many no longer believe in science in quite the way they used to. Yes, if theories in physics work, use them. But let's not claim for them more than we should. Certainly, there is no way we want to lose all the good that has come from the huge success of modern science. There can be no return to the Dark Ages. But at the end of the day, science is not everything.

The bubble has burst

The bubble of scientific confidence and trust in reason has burst. Nor is this only because of philosophical problems; this loss of confidence is increased by an attendant, felt lack of meaning. This is now a fact in Western culture. It has for long been reflected in films, plays and novels.

In the late fifties it surfaced in the Theatre of the Absurd. This came from a sense of disillusionment and a collapse of all previously held firm beliefs. Here is the assessment of Martin Esslin writing his introduction to the Penguin *Absurd Drama* in 1965:

> The social and spiritual reasons for such a sense of loss of meaning are manifold and complex; the waning of religious faith that had started with the Enlightenment and led Nietzsche to speak of the 'death of God' by the eighteen-eighties; the breakdown of the liberal faith in inevitable social progress in the wake of the First World War; the disillusionment with the hopes of radical social revolution as predicted by Marx after Stalin had turned the Soviet Union into a totalitarian tyranny; the relapse into barbarism, mass murder, and genocide in the course of Hitler's brief rule over Europe during the Second World War; and, in the aftermath of that war, the spread of spiritual emptiness in the outwardly prosperous and affluent societies of Western Europe and the United States. There can be no doubt: for many intelligent and sensitive human beings the world of the mid twentieth century *had* lost its meaning and simply ceased to make sense. Previously held certainties have dissolved, the firmest foundations for hope and optimism have collapsed. Suddenly man sees himself faced with a universe that is both frightening and illogical — in a word, absurd.[9]

Three years later in 1968 there were the student barricades in Paris. Indeed, there was a worldwide student revolt. One journalist described it as 'not a mere generation conflict. Nor is it just a fight for University reform — not any more. It is a total onslaught on modern industrial society.'

And by now the war in Vietnam was raging, a war that showed the futility and bankruptcy of both East and West.

All the moral values were turned upside down. The Americans were championing 'freedom'. But what that meant was clean-shaven young men having to fly off from their sanitized aircraft carriers to blast Vietnamese peasants into eternity. It meant the free use of napalm. But were the Viet Cong any better? Of course not. They seemed just as brutal, cunning and inhuman. Vietnam had no winners.

So was this the high point of the Enlightenment?

Religious revival in the United States

Many saw the need for a complete rethink, especially in the United States. The preaching of Billy Graham and the growth of the Pentecostal movement were essential background to religious revival. But reactions against, or at least questions about, Vietnam more than anything else sparked off a religious revival in the United States. This has been going on ever since and is part of the church growth we mentioned earlier.

The Jesus Revolution of the early seventies was a flamboyant expression of something that was (and is) going much deeper. At the time of the Jesus Revolution, Chuck Smith, the Pentecostal pastor of a small 150-strong chapel, took pity on the drop-outs and hippies on the beaches of Los Angeles. Against the cultural background we have been describing, a 'landslide' occurred: huge numbers were converted to Jesus Christ. Chuck Smith's church within ten years became a church attended each Sunday by thousands. It has spawned over 100 daughter churches. Many other churches were affected by the Jesus Revolution. Something had changed in the Christian consciousness in the United States.

For many in America, Vietnam meant that not all of the Enlightenment was good. Some of its values, as well as some of its achievements in the twentieth century, were under judgement. If the end-product was to drop on a tiny Asian country in one year more bombs than were dropped on Europe in the whole of the Second World War, who wanted that?

The American historian, Theodore Roszak, in an important book *The Making of a Counter Culture* put it like this in 1968:

> The life of Reason (with a capital R) has all too obviously failed to bring us the agenda of civilized improvements the Voltaires and Condorcets once foresaw. Indeed, Reason, material Progress, the scientific world view have revealed themselves in numerous respects as simply a higher superstition, based on dubious but well concealed assumptions about man and nature. Science, it has been said, thrives on sins of omission. True enough; and for three hundred years, those omissions have been piling up rather like the slag tips that surround Welsh mining towns: immense, precipitous mountains of frustrated human aspiration which threaten dangerously to come cascading down in an impassioned landslide. It is quite impossible any longer to ignore the fact that our conception of intellect has been narrowed disastrously by the prevailing assumption, especially in the academies, that the life of the spirit is: (1) a lunatic fringe best left to artists and marginal visionaries; (2) an historical boneyard for antiquarian scholarship; (3) a highly specialized adjunct of professional anthropology; (4) an antiquated vocabulary still used by the clergy, but intelligently soft-pedaled by its more enlightened members.[10]

9

Crisis in the Church of England

The fundamental issue facing the Church of England and the other mainline Protestant denominations is not the Virgin Birth and the Empty Tomb. These doctrines raise very important questions. But in one sense the Virgin Birth and the Empty Tomb can be seen as presenting problems or symptoms.

The real issue is this: is the leadership of the Church willing to face two facts — first, the fact that we are living in a post-Enlightenment world in the West; and secondly, the fact that many of the younger clergy and laity (and therefore the potential future leaders of the Church) have *already* decided that there is no future in Modernist liberal Protestantism; and these people are *already* going in the direction of a full-blooded apostolic Christianity and thus are diametrically opposed to much in the current leadership of the Church? Let us look at these two facts in more detail.

The melting of an iceberg

First, we must remember that the United Kingdom has not had a 'Vietnam'. It has not had the opportunity of being jolted out of the Enlightenment. It is moving much more slowly. That is significant, for in the United States as a result of Vietnam an authentic and popular religious consciousness was awakened. It signalled the beginning of the end of the Enlightenment. What is more, it elected two American presidents! First, there was the Democratic Jimmy Carter, whose electoral appeal was that he was a 'born-again' Christian. No President this century had run on a 'born-again' ticket! Second, there was the Republican Ronald Reagan, who then defeated Carter. Reagan had the support of better organized right-wing religious groups. But religion was now out in the public forum in an unprecedented way.

In the United Kingdom there has been no sudden awakening like this. There has been no Vietnam. But Enlightenment arrogance is tiring and religious consciousness is awakening gradually, and it is becoming public in the current controversy over the Bishop of Durham and the other 'doubting bishops'. As the Bishop of Durham has described himself, he is a 'sociological event' — but not in the way he might think! For the doubting bishops represent a tired humanism that is already out of date. The Bishop of Durham represents a Canute-like attempt to stem the tide of change. But because he is personally so very warmhearted and expressive, because certain political issues (upon which Modernists and the orthodox agree) have got involved, and because the doctrinal debate is seen by some simply as a matter of theology (and esoteric theology at that), *the real issues can be missed*. However, something highly significant is going on. We can liken it to the melting of an iceberg. The iceberg is the Enlightenment. The tip of the iceberg is the denial of the Virgin Birth and the doubting of the Empty Tomb. The warm water is made up of three components. First, the surge of Christian sentiment around the country against these doubts and denials; second, the interest of the media often bewildered by the extravagant utterances of some of the bishops; and, third, the knowledge that things are very different in growing churches in other parts of the world. None of this will elect a Prime Minister (yet). But it is significant. It shows that there are bishops who are out of step with many of their clergy and people. It shows also that they are out of step with the non-religious world. Indeed, that world is confused. It does not know what it believes. However, it knows that it doesn't believe in Enlightenment humanism. After all, what could be less like the Enlightenment or humanism than contemporary punk rock? The extreme radicalism in both the Church and the nation mustn't blind us to the underlying spiritual situation.

On the one hand

The second fact the leadership of the Church of England must face is this. For a number of years now, 50 per cent of the ordinands coming out of the theological colleges of the Church of England have been coming from the Evangelical colleges. A proportion of the rest are committed Anglo-Catholics. This body of men have long rejected the teaching of Modernist bishops. They see it as being in grave error as a matter of theology; and also they see it as irrelevant to the needs of the late twentieth century.

This group broadly speaking agrees with Lesslie Newbigin's analysis of our present predicament, when he says:

> At the risk of over-simplification one may say that while the Roman Catholic Church put up defensive barriers against the Enlightenment, the Protestant churches gradually surrendered the public sphere to control by the assumptions of the Enlightenment and survived by retreating into the private sector. The typical form of living Christian faith in its Protestant forms from the eighteenth century onwards was pietism, a religion of the soul, of the inner life, of personal morals and of the home.[1]

And the overall result of the Church's compromise with the Enlightenment has led to what can be fairly called syncretism. 'It would be hard to deny,' writes Newbigin, 'that contemporary British (and most of western) Christianity is an advanced case of syncretism.'[2]

The Church of England (together with the other Protestant churches) is thus incapable of either challenging the lifestyle or the intellectual framework of the modern world because it has so absorbed both the values and ideas of the world around. It is truly a 'worldly' Church.

In the current debate within the Church of England there is thus a struggle going on of the very greatest historical significance.

On the one hand there are those in the Church of England who believe that their communities and the nation need and want to hear clearly the gospel of God: that he is Lord of all; that he has purposes for nations as well as individuals; that he visits and redeems his people; that men and women need saving; that his kingdom has begun in dramatic fashion with the death and Resurrection of Jesus; and that one day Jesus Christ will return 'to judge both the living and the dead'.

These are the 'building blocks' that the late twentieth and early twenty-first centuries can use, they believe, to re-fashion a culture. For, they say quite rightly, we need to work out policies and plans for public as well as for private life, using quite explicitly the values of the Christian faith. They are convinced that there is a desperate need for this to happen. There indeed needs to be a measure of de-secularization in society. Our own society could easily end up in social breakdown through a loss of purpose, meaning and values. We are under threat. Many would even argue we are experiencing judgement in the Church and in the nation. The Church has so singularly failed to preach, and the nation has for so long failed to respond to, the gospel of Jesus and his Resurrection. We should not, therefore, be surprised if we face social, political and economic problems. Repent-ance, however, has to begin with the Church.

Nor are these people crying out for a new obscurantism. They are willing to admit that they do not have all the answers. They admit that some of the answers they have given to the problems thrown up by the study of the Bible, the modern sciences, and public and private ethics are only tentative, that some are inadequate, others provisional and many, possibly, are in need of revision. But they maintain that they have been attempting to give *Christian* answers and not *sub-Christian* answers.

On the other hand

On the other hand there are those in the current leadership of the Church who believe that the way to commend the Christian faith is to have 'more of the same' as we have been having (in some measure) since the Enlightenment. Instead of interpreting the secular mind in the light of the gospel, they want to interpret the gospel in the light of the secular mind. So bishops are addressing their Diocesan Synods and writing in their Diocesan Newsletters in this vein, no doubt with the best of intentions and motives. But the effect is to cast doubt on the Virgin Birth, the Empty Tomb, petitionary prayer and to discredit significant elements in the Bible and the tradition of the Christian Church. There is the apparent assumption that if you knock off a few (or all) of the miracles and we get back to a simple Deism, with Jesus a very holy Jew, people will believe. They seem to be saying, 'Of course, if you are a Hindu or a Muslim, we won't bother you because all religions get there in the end.'

It is classical Modernism. But there is no way that, in the long term, this Modernism and apostolic Christianity can coexist. Here the Roman Catholic Church was right. Nor is this a denial of Anglican comprehensiveness. This is not a disagreement about secondary matters but about fundamentals. The gospel miracles of the Virgin Birth and the Resurrection are fundamental.

It was C. S. Lewis who said you can't strip Christianity of the miraculous:

> In a religion like Buddhism, if you took away the miracles attributed to Gautama Buddha in some very late sources, there would be no loss; in fact, the religion would get on very much better without them because in that case the miracles largely contradict the teaching. Or even in the case of a religion like Mohammedanism, nothing essential would be altered if you took away the miracles. You could have a great prophet preaching his dogmas without bringing in any miracles; they are only in the

nature of a digression, or illuminated capitals. But you cannot possible do that with Christianity, because the Christian story is precisely the story of one grand miracle, the Christian assertion being that what is beyond all space and time, what is uncreated, eternal, came into nature, into human nature, descended into His own universe, and rose again, bringing nature up with Him.[3]

The tragedy is that those in the leadership supporting these modernistic ideas are supporting a cause without a future. Because of the 'closed circuitry' and narrow introspection of academic theology, they can so easily be blissfully unaware of this fact.

Moreover, the media coverage given to current episcopal doubts must not be misconstrued. Since Easter 1984 denials of the Virgin Birth and doubts over the Empty Tomb have regularly hit the headlines. The Church has indeed become a talking point. But that by itself proves nothing. There certainly is a raw nerve of religious consciousness in the nation that can be exposed. Christianity is of deep interest to more than regular church attenders. But unless religious needs are going to be met, the current debate will simply be the newsworthiness of religious conflict. This is how it was in the sixties — the generation of the Bishop of Woolwich's book *Honest to God*, the New Morality and the Death of God theology. But where is all that now? Where are the ideas now of Thomas J. J. Altizer, William Hamilton and Alistair Kee? Where even are Paul Tillich's? Media coverage of the New Theology in the sixties did not herald the growth of the Church but rather increasing decline! Media coverage of the 'doubting bishops' similarly will prove nothing unless there is a willingness for the Church of England's current leadership to face the facts. Obviously bishops who appear to deny the fundamentals of the Christian faith are news for the moment. But in the long term where will they be and where will they lead the Church?

The run-up to the crisis

The crisis that came to a head in July 1984 came about because the Archbishop of York consecrated a man as a bishop in the Church of England who had publicly denied the Virgin Birth and doubted the Empty Tomb. Never before had this happened. On a previous occasion this century Hensley Henson was suspected of similar denials and doubts. But before his consecration as a bishop, the Archbishop of Canterbury required certain assurances. These were given and Henson was consecrated in 1918. In this way the Church of England made it clear that its bishops may not deny or doubt these fundamental doctrines of the Christian faith. But John Habgood, the present Archbishop of York, unilaterally reversed this policy of the Church of England, by going ahead with the consecration of David Jenkins.

However, we can trace this crisis over the new Bishop of Durham's consecration directly back to August 1921. It was then that Dr Burge, the Bishop of Oxford, first approached Randall Davidson, the Archbishop of Canterbury, about setting up a Doctrine Commission. He was the spokesman on behalf of a number of prominent Church leaders. They saw the danger signals from growing doctrinal division. But they still believed that (to quote the words of G. K. H. Bell, the Archbishop's biographer):

All but a comparatively small number of extremists of each school could reach agreement, both on the essentials of the Christian faith and on the points of controversy which had bitterly divided them in the past.[4]

The need for such a conference was underlined by the Conference of Modern Churchmen held at Girton College, Cambridge, the same month — August 1921. Some of the speakers openly cast doubt on the Virgin Birth. Hastings Rashdall argued that you could 'insulate' the Incarnation from the Virgin Birth. He also redefined the Incarnation as meaning that Christ was the most Godlike man that has ever lived. There was uproar in the Church.

So in 1922 an official letter asking for a Doctrine Commission was sent by nine Diocesan bishops, seventeen senior clergy and one layman to the Archbishop of Canterbury. They were desperately concerned that the doctrinal disagreements were not only wasting time but leading to Church decline:

> Controversy weakens the loyalty of individuals and their sense of obligation to the Church of which they are members, and it renders the Church as a whole powerless to give her proper witness in the political and social difficulties of the present time.[5]

This group were facing reality. They knew there might be 'differences of so irremovable a character as to render impossible anything but a purely artificial and external unity based on the fact of the Establishment rather than on agreement in belief.'[6] But they were hoping that differences would be over secondary matters. They realized that the secession of some was a real danger. But they foresaw a more damaging split in the Church:

> It is becoming increasingly clear that the only adequate safeguard against far more serious disruption lies not in the fact of the Establishment, but in securing a genuine unity of belief.[7]

And for them the supreme problem was pastoral:

> Again, it is of almost primary importance to solve the actual pastoral problem which is presented by directly contradictory teaching in different parishes in respect of doctrines which are closely bound up with the devotional life of all Christians. Such contradictions often affect disastrously the religious life of individuals. They constitute also a graver obstacle than is ordinarily recognized to the evangelization of the nation.[8]

On December 28th 1922 a Doctrine Commission was set up. It was *not* to be prescriptive — saying what the Church of England's doctrine *should* be, but descriptive — saying what people actually *were* believing. The Archbishop of Canterbury wrote that it 'should not be an authoritative statement, but that it should, when prepared, be laid before the Bishops for them to consider what further action (if any) should be taken.'[9] The first meeting of the Commission was held at

University College, Oxford in September 1923.

Fifteen years later

The Commission reported fifteen years later in 1938! By this time William Temple, Archbishop of York, was Chairman.

The storm clouds were gathering over Europe. The whole fabric of Western civilization was under threat from Hitler on the one hand and Stalin on the other. The United Kingdom had hardly got out of recession. There were the marital problems of King Edward VIII, and the government was weak. In Germany a large part of the Church was being corrupted in the interests of Nazism, and religious exiles — especially Jews — had already settled in England.

It was at such a time as this that the Doctrine Commission decided to let loose on the country a document that *seemed* to suggest that in the Church of England it was all right to deny the Virgin Birth and doubt the Empty Tomb of Jesus.

The Press had a field day. Clergy were scandalized. A petition was signed by 8,000 clergy — nearly half the ordained clergy of the Church of England of all parties. True, the Anglo-Catholics had initiated the proceedings. But others joined in. And there were motions in the Convocations.

In the Convocation of York there was a motion sent by the clergy to the Bishops asking them to declare:

> (1) That the doctrine set forth in the Book of Common Prayer and the Thirty-nine Articles of Religion remains the authoritative teaching of the Church of England.
> (2) That the Church of England holds and teaches the Nicene Creed, in that sense only in which it has ever been held throughout the history of the Church, and that her ministers cannot rightly claim a liberty to set aside by private interpretation the historic meaning of those clauses which state the events of the earthly life of our Lord Jesus Christ.[10]

This motion was proposed by the Rev. E. W. Kemp, who said in his speech:

> The clergy at the present time have enough matters of anxiety to

meet without having to meet this added anxiety of facing . . . the great difficulty that within the Church there are accredited teachers denying the great fundamental truths of the Gospel faith.[11]

Clergy from the working-class parishes were particularly disturbed. Canon Kerby spoke on behalf of working-class parishes in the Manchester Diocese. He said that he and other clergy had been urged by the Bishop and other people in authority to get on with the work of evangelism. 'But,' he said, 'we are beginning to wonder what is the Gospel we have to preach, and what is the faith to which we have to try to win people.'

He added: 'There is no getting over the fact that the manner in which the report has been issued has caused widespread trouble and difficulty among the ordinary rank and file of the community.' Then there was the problem of church growth. Canon Kerby said that while the Church was deploring that the number of her adherents was going down at a tremendously rapid rate, they were being continuously held up by these documents which intellectuals were producing. Sometimes they were tempted almost to despair in their endeavours to forward the work they had been commissioned to perform; and while naturally he was prepared to value all that the theological intellectuals contributed to the Church by their thought and by their minds, at the same time he did wish they would give the Church, for ten years at any rate, a rest, so that they could get on with their proper work of saving souls![12]

The 1938 Doctrine Report

A number of Anglican bishops, clergy and lay people have been given to understand that the Doctrine Report of 1938 sets the limits for the Doctrine of the Church of England. You are therefore allowed to deny the Virgin Birth and doubt the Empty Tomb and be an accredited teacher in the Church. That is quite wrong. The Report did not set limits. Rather what it did was to raise a number of questions about doctrine in the Church of England. These were never answered. They are in the process of being answered in the current debate over doctrine in the Church of England. As there is considerable confusion about it in the Church of England, we must spell this out in some detail.

Not the Doctrine of the Church of England

There was a problem over the presentation of the Report. The 1938 Doctrine Commission Report had been launched without proper warning or a special note to the effect that, one, this was *not* a statement of the Doctrine of the Church of England; two, it had no authoritative force; three, it was simply descriptive; and, four, its title was 'Doctrine *in* the Church of England' and not 'Doctrine *of* the Church of England'.

But the damage was done; and since that time many bishops, as we have said, have thought that this Report determines the limits of what is doctrinally permissible today. The Bishop of Newcastle said this to the Newcastle Diocese, just before the Consecration of David Jenkins whom he was going to present in York Minster:

> With regard to the clauses concerning the Virgin Birth and the Resurrection, it seems to me that there has been granted, at any rate tacitly by our Church, considerable room for liberty of interpretation, at least since the publication of the report *Doctrine in the Church of England* 46 years ago, before some of us were born. We believe them to be true, for they are part of the package handed on to us by the Church: we are allowed liberty of interpretation with regard to the sense in which they are true, whether they are true for instance, historically or theologically or poetically or in analogical manner or in more than one of these senses.[1]

But this is wrong. The doctrine of the Church of England is determined by its Constitution, and that means Canon A.5. The importance of this Canon has been underlined by *The Church of England (Worship and Doctrine) Measure 1974.* This says in section 5 (1):

> References in this Measure to the doct.ine of the Church of England shall be construed in accordance with the statement concerning that doctrine contained in the Canons of the Church of England, which statement is in the following terms: 'the doctrine of the Church of England is grounded in the holy Scriptures, and in such teachings of the ancient Fathers and Councils of the Church as are agreeable to the said Scriptures. In particular such doctrine is to be found in the Thirty-nine Articles of Religion, the Book of Common Prayer, and the Ordinal.'

Temple's regret

William Temple, the Chairman of the Commission, knew this Report was not determining doctrine. He was worried that others would fail to realize this. He said:

> I have one regret, and that is that I did not see how desirable it would be, as I now see it would have been desirable, to secure that at the outset of the document when published there should be a note, either from the Archbishop of Canterbury or from the

two Archbishops together, saying what is stated very plainly in the report, by saying it all alone so that it would stand out, namely, that the report of the Commission is a setting forth of what they found to be the prevailing currents of thought and teaching within the Church at the present time, and *not a declaration of the authoritative teaching of the Church in its corporate capacity*.[2] [Italics mine.]

Indeed, the Report had opened with a repeat of the terms of reference, as outlined in 1922. It repeats the very words of the Archbishop of Canterbury's briefing letter (written on behalf of himself and the Archbishop of York) to the Bishop of Oxford:

We note and approve your proposal that the Report of the Commission *should not be an authoritative statement,* but that it should, when prepared, be laid before the Bishops for them to consider what further action (if any) should be taken.[3]

What could be clearer?

So important did William Temple think this was that in his own 'Chairman's Introduction' he had written this:

Our terms of reference, as set out in the letter of Archbishop Davidson to Bishop Bruge, did not include the question what varieties of doctrine or of interpretation are to be regarded as permissible in the Church of England.[4]

And Temple was quite clear that the doctrine of the Church of England was not an amalgam of the beliefs of the clergy. The mere fact that some clergymen within the Church of England might be denying the Virgin Birth or doubting the Empty Tomb did not mean that the doctrine of the Church of England was therefore affected.

He realized that there were two questions about what is permissible in the Church of England. He distinguished between what is permissible as the doctrine of the Church of England and what is permissible before one is *excluded* from the Church of England:

It is therefore important to emphasize the distinction between the judgment that such-and-such an opinion is incompatible with the Christian faith or the Anglican tradition, and the judgment that such-and-such a person, who holds an opinion thus condemned, should be excluded from the exercise of office or of membership in the Church.[5]

The Virgin Birth and the Empty Tomb in the Report

But what did the Report actually say? It had this to say about the Virgin Birth:

> The main grounds on which the doctrine is valued are the following. It is a safeguard of the Christian conviction that in the birth of Jesus we have, not simply the birth of a new individual of the human species, but the advent of One who 'for us men and for our salvation came down from heaven.' It is congruous with the belief that in the Person of Christ humanity made a fresh beginning. It coheres with the supernatural element in the life of Christ, indicating a unique inauguration of that unique life. It gives expression to the idea of the response of the human race to God's purpose through the obedience and faith of the Blessed Virgin Mary.
>
> Many of us hold, accordingly, that belief in the Word made flesh *is integrally bound up with* belief in the Virgin Birth, and that this will increasingly be recognised.
>
> There are, however, some among us who hold that a full belief in the historical incarnation is more consistent with the supposition that our Lord's birth took place under the normal conditions of human generation. In their minds the notion of a Virgin Birth tends to mar the completeness of the belief that in the Incarnation God revealed Himself at every point in and through human nature.[6]

Many on the Commission believed in the Virgin Birth; some didn't.

With regard to the Resurrection the question was asked, 'What was it exactly that happened?' The Report said:

> A variety of answers is possible. Belief that the Lord was risen — the acceptance of the *kerygma* itself — is compatible both with a realisation that we cannot expect to reach clear or full knowledge in detail, and also with a variety of critical views. If a general principle is to be laid down, we may say that the Christian faith is compatible with all such critical reconstructions of the events underlying the narratives as would not have the effect, if ac-

cepted, of invalidating the apostolic testimony to Jesus as the Lord who rose from the dead. To speak more positively, we are of the opinion that it ought to be affirmed that Jesus was veritably alive and victorious; that He showed Himself alive from the dead, to the disciples; and that the fact of His rising, however explained (and it involves probably an element beyond our explaining), is to be understood to have been an event as real and concrete as the crucifixion itself (which it reversed) and an act of God, wholly unique in human history. The symbol of this fact in the Gospels is the story of the empty tomb. More than one explanation of this has been suggested; but the majority of the Commission are agreed in holding the traditional explanation — viz. that the tomb was empty because the Lord had risen.[7]

When this was read many of the clergy in the Church of England saw it as a house built on sand. It was an elegant statement. But if the Empty Tomb is only to be believed as a symbol, the pass has been sold! How could the Crucifixion be 'reversed' if the remains of Jesus are still in the soil of Palestine? No wonder Alan Stephenson has said that when the report came out 'it was greeted by Modernists as a victory for their party.' But the Church at large was not taken in.

Clearly these statements on the Virgin Birth and the Empty Tomb marked huge disagreement. But was this disagreement in the realm of *optional* doctrine?

The importance of the Virgin Birth and the Empty Tomb

When William Temple addressed himself to the question of the Resurrection, he made it clear that he did not believe the Empty Tomb to be optional. In this he was unlike many of today's bishops. He believed it *mattered* whether you believed in the Empty Tomb or not. Referring to the two groups — the majority who believed and the minority who didn't, he said to the Bishops at York:

> When two bodies of people state views of that sort, it is not reasonable to say that all of them are agreed in saying that it does not matter: one group say it does; another say it does not.

And William Temple (with the majority believed that the

traditional view on the Empty Tomb 'would be increasingly recognized as congruous with and cohering with the whole belief of the Church.'[8]

Temple knew of the seriousness of the situation. So unlike some of today's bishops who will not state their own convictions, Temple felt it important to say this:

> In view of my own responsibility in the Church I think it right here to affirm that I wholeheartedly accept as historical facts the birth of our Lord from a virgin mother and the resurrection of his physical body from death and the tomb.[9]

But Temple also realized that doctrinal disagreements could not for ever be unresolved. There was a point at which 'spiritual fellowship is endangered'. He said the hope was that:

> The utmost liberty of thought compatible with maintenance of spiritual fellowship should be secured. But what is the precise point at which spiritual fellowship is endangered, and by what methods those who endanger it should be restrained, are questions that lie outside our province.[10]

The Bishops in 1938 wanted to allay confusion. At York in June of that year, where William Temple himself was President of the Convocation, the Bishops passed a motion on the Doctrine Report which included these words:

> This House [of Bishops] . . . recognises that the report neither is nor claims to be a declaration of the doctrine of the Church — a purpose lying outside the Commission's terms of reference and one for which no Commission appointed as this was could be competent.

And the concluding words of the Bishops' motion were very important:

> Inasmuch as many have misunderstood the function of this Commission as explained above, this House, while recognising the reality of the problems which scholars and theologians are handling, and desiring to maintain in the Church the fullest freedom of enquiry which is compatible with spiritual fellowship, thinks well to state that the doctrine of the Church of England is now, as it has been in the past time, the doctrine set forth in the Creeds, in the Prayer Book, and in the Articles of Religion.[11]

Asking too much

In January 1939 the Bishops discussed the second part of the motion the Clergy had earlier sent to them. The clergy wanted the Bishops to declare 'that the Church of England holds and teaches the Nicene Creed, in that sense only in which it has ever been held throughout the history of the Church.' That, of course, was asking for the impossible. William Temple pointed out that the detailed teaching of the clauses of the Creeds had varied over the centuries. For example at some periods in the Church's history it was the fact that Jesus was *born* of the Virgin Mary that had to be emphasized — that he was truly man. Obviously interpretation on all the many different parts of the Nicene Creed has varied. For example the Creed says: 'He will come again in glory to judge the living and the dead . . . We look for the resurrection of the dead.' But from the early Fathers on, there were different interpretations of the details of these clauses. So 'to hold and teach the Nicene Creed (in toto) in that sense only in which it has ever been held throughout the history of the Church' is impossible.

The Bishops therefore passed a resolution in these terms:

> The history of the Church supplies much evidence of the unwisdom of any attempt to limit interpretation by authoritative declaration: we are convinced that the wise course is not to prescribe the interpretation in addition to the standard itself.[12]

In November 1984, in Question Time in the General Synod, the Archbishop of Canterbury, Robert Runcie, cited this motion in an answer to a question. He was being asked to refer to the House of Bishops

> for a clear answer by the Bishops the questions raised by clergy in the north east of England, namely:
>
> a) do they agree or not that a bishop may disbelieve in the historicity of the Virgin Birth and the Empty Tomb?
>
> b) do they disagree or not that a bishop may be agnostic about the historicity of the Virgin Birth and the Empty Tomb?
>
> c) do they agree or not that a bishop, while himself believing in the historicity of the Virgin Birth and the Empty Tomb, may

treat and teach these beliefs as being optional for the Church?

The Archbishop agreed to the request but then quoted the resolution of the bishops at York in 1939: 'The history of the Church supplies much evidence of the unwisdom of any attempt to limit interpretation [of doctrinal standards] by authoritative declaration etc.'

But the arguments of the bishops in 1939 were exclusively and *only* about limiting interpretation of the Nicene Creed as a whole. The Church should not prescribe a complete interpretation of *all* the clauses of the Creed.

But the Church of England already has set limits on *specific* clauses of the Creed. Article IV of the Thirty-nine Articles indicates that the Resurrection should not be reinterpreted to deny the Empty Tomb.

However, in January 1939 it was a pity that the Clergy had asked the Bishops for too much. It enabled the Bishops to shelve these fundamental problems.

The 1938 Doctrine Report had created further doctrinal confusion. The Doctrine Commission had failed. The reason for its inception in 1922 was to promote unity. The Church was now more divided than ever.

The Bishops, however, would not be able to shelve these problems for ever. For it was the Roman Catholic Modernist Father Tyrell, writing to Cardinal Mercier, who said: 'where [doctrinal] diversity is accepted as final and satisfactory, there can be no progress, but only an aimless analysis and disintegration.'[13]

The intervening years

The Second World War came to the Bishops rescue! Hitler made shelving these problems easy.

But modernistic, liberal Protestantism was on the wane. Archbishop William Temple became Archbishop of Canterbury; and the year before he died, together with the Archbishop of York, he set up a Commission on Evangelism under the Bishop of Rochester, Christopher Chavasse. Its

Report was published in 1945 under the title *Towards the Conversion of England*. It was a best seller, with the first edition being sold overnight. It was a good report with much that is still relevant, but it did not gain general acceptance. This was not surprising now that the new Archbishop of Canterbury, Geoffrey Fisher, was not really behind it. However, it was of profound importance in that it created a climate of confidence for some younger men who were beginning to appear — the new Evangelicals.

But the Church of England hardly realized what was happening. It seemed to be ignoring the significance of the rebirth of Evangelicalism. This was because for the next twenty years its main energies were taken up with Canon Law Revision.

In May 1947 Archbishop Fisher said:

> The reform of Canon Law is, I believe the first and most essential step in the whole process of Church reform . . . Because we have no body of Canons to turn to, the Church has lost its sense of obedience to its own spiritual ordinances.[14]

This in itself was a blow for Modernism after the success of 1938. In 1956 Henry Major retired after forty-six years as Editor of the *Modern Churchman*. On his retirement he wrote to the new President of the Modern Churchman's Union, Clifford Rhodes, saying that Modernists should try to ensure 'that the Revised Canons be not legalised nor be claimed to possess legal authority' and 'that the Revised Canons be not imposed on the clergy or included in any form of subscription required from them.'[15] But the Canons became law in 1969 and Canon A.5 now defines the Doctrine of the Church of England and quite clearly that Canon implies that the Virgin Birth and the Empty Tomb are part of the Doctrine of the Church of England. These Canons, of course, were not available in 1938, nor earlier when Hensley Henson was consecrated a bishop. But these are the Canons the new Bishop of Durham was consecrated under.

However, the Virgin Birth and the Empty Tomb did not

feature in the central debates of the Church of England over this period. This may have been because in the main doctrinal controversy in the sixties — the *Honest to God* controversy, Bishop John Robinson did not challenge the Empty Tomb. In fact he was a stalwart defender of the Empty Tomb.[16] The issue was more over our 'image of God'.

Nor did these two fundamental doctrines feature in the debates in the seventies. For during this period the General Synod was all absorbed in revising services and producing the new Alternative Services Book.

It is true that another Doctrine Commission produced a report in 1976 entitled *Christian Believing*.[17] This showed how sick the Church of England was doctrinally. The report was disregarded and not even given a hearing in the General Synod. The Archbishop of York (still then Bishop of Durham) spoke in favour of it at the York Convocation. But there were members of the Convocation who considered much of it outright heresy. That was not surprising as the Chairman of the Commission was Professor Maurice Wiles, who together with Professor Nineham (also a Doctrine Commission member!) was about to contribute to a volume of essays entitled *The Myth of God Incarnate*.[18] This was published in 1977 and was seen by many as a denial of the deity of Christ. The effect of all this was that Doctrine Commissions lost all credibility in the wider Church. The situation was not really redeemed by a new chairman being appointed, the Bishop of Winchester, John V. Taylor. In 1981 a report was published under his chairmanship entitled *Believing in the Church*.[19] The damage had been done. The popular perception was that liberal academic theology in the Church of England was so *sub-Christian*, and self-evidently so, that the Church could not even be angered by doctrinal heresy. The reports were an irrelevance. That is why for the majority the doctrinal issues were as they had been left in 1938. And that is why David Jenkins has had such a hearing. He has opened up the issues of 1938 again.

11

Current leadership

David Jenkins, the Bishop of Durham, has in a sense done the Church of England a service in forcing the Church, and in particular the House of Bishops, to pick up the pieces as they were left in 1938. The issues of the Virgin Birth and the Empty Tomb were then shelved. They have become again the centre of debate and controversy.

But if liberal Protestantism and Modernism is on the wane, how is it that there are so many in the current leadership of the Church who are of this persuasion? And how is it they have a certain following? In part it is their 'age'.

The 'doubting bishops' are really 'yesterday's men', for they are typical Modernists who deny the Virgin Birth and doubt the Empty Tomb but affirm the Incarnation. And from one point of view that position can be said to be something of the past.

The decline of the Modern Churchmen's Union

Typical or older Modernism went sharply into decline after the Somerville Conference of the Modern Churchmen's Union in 1967. There Professor Nineham spoke on *Jesus in the Gospels*. He was saying that it is

> Possible to hold that Jesus was genuinely, limitedly and confusedly human . . . and yet to hold that God was uniquely active in and through him . . . In that case much of what the later Christians said

124

about Jesus, the Virgin Birth and the ever more exalted titles they attributed to him, would fail to be seen as expressions, more or less adequate to their time and place, of their developing realization of what a unique and truly wonderful work God had begun through him.[1]

As Alan Stephenson wrote in the *Church Times:*

Where do we go from here? If Nineham is right, then Christology will have to receive a far more radical treatment than this Conference gave it. Indeed, we shall have to talk about 'the event of Christ' rather than 'the person of Christ'.[2]

How right he was. The logic of the Modernist position, following the exegesis of Dennis Nineham, was to adopt the New Radicalism of *The Myth of God Incarnate* which was published ten years later.

This publication was just one indication that typical or older '1938 Modernism' had been replaced by the Radicalism of Professor Wiles and others, which is so blatantly Deist if not atheist and, therefore, should not really be called Christian. In fact Wiles explicitly admits his position is deistic. He says it is 'deistic in so far as it refrains from claiming any effective causation on the part of God in relation to particular occurrences.'[3]

So the older Modernists were pushed out of the scene by the New Radicals. The older Modernists clearly were not happy with what was emerging from their wing of theology. Stephenson reports on the Somerville Conference that it was quite divided: 'The older members, and hence the majority, sided with the more conservative speakers, the younger ones with Nineham.'[4] But the logic is with Wiles, Nineham and Cupitt. For *if you are going to adopt a sub-Christian way of doing theology,* in the end you will end up with something that is sub-Christian. That is why a number of people pulled back from Modernism as it was evolving in such an extreme direction.

One paper by a younger participant at the Somerville Conference asked whether Jesus was a homosexual — although there was no suggestion that Jesus was a practising homosexual.[5] Even so, many felt this was in very bad taste. And all this meant that the younger Radicals were identified as 'the lunatic fringe' of the Modern Churchmen's Union. The older element 'pulled back' (and then died off!) leaving a very weak and divided Modern Churchmen's Union.

Many were, therefore, taken by surprise seventeen years later at the re-emergence of a spirited Modernist in the form of the new Bishop of Durham. By pushing his views so publicly he has forced a number of other bishops to admit agreement. These bishops previously appeared quite happy to 'lie low' and ride out their time, consciously or subconsciously realizing that things were changing.

There was a common perception in the Church of England that the new Radicals were too extreme by half. And people of the older Modernist school realized they couldn't compete with a new force that was coming onto the Anglican scene (and more importantly the worldwide Church scene) — a renewed Evangelicalism. Thus the strength of the Modern Churchmen's Union following the Somerville Conference in 1967 has dwindled.

Modern Evangelicals

Ever since that time in 1967, when another conference was being held at Keele University, the strength of Evangelicals in the Church of England has been growing quite remarkably. This followed major growth of Evangelicalism among students with the result that there have been more and more Evangelical ordinands. In the late fifties and early sixties John Stott, the Rector of All Souls', Langham Place, London, was an important figure in these student circles.

Other people, however, at this time made their mark. David Sheppard (now Bishop of Liverpool) helped these (often) middle-class Evangelical students to be aware of the social dimension of the gospel as it affected the inner cities through his work at the Mayflower Family Centre in Canning Town, London. Dick Lucas from St Helen's in Bishopsgate, London, started leading university missions. In the late sixties and through into the seventies David Watson and David MacInnes (once a fellow curate with David Watson in Gillingham) had a profound effect on the student world. All this led to a significant growth of the Inter-Varsity Fellowship (now the Universities and Colleges Christian Fellowship).

But parallel with the growth of the Christian Union movement, a new confidence was growing in the Evangelical parishes and in the Evangelical theological colleges. After the 1967 Keele Evangelical Anglican Congress, came the 1977 Nottingham Evangelical Anglican Congress.

Furthermore, worldwide there was a growth in Evangelicalism. This lead to the Lausanne Congress on World Evangelization in 1974. The Papers and the Responses of the Congress have been published as *Let the Earth Hear His Voice*,[6] and show that the worldwide Evangelical movement is probably the most significant movement in contemporary Christianity. Now more confident in its theology, it is properly concerned with church growth, evangelism and social action.

But modern Evangelicalism cannot be fully understood apart from the Renewal Movement. This began as a reaction to what was seen as the over-cerebral interests of some of the new Evangelicals. For this was a time for a mushrooming of Evangelical scholarship. But some weren't totally convinced that the kingdom of God would come through more and more Ph.D. programmes.

In the Church of England it is undoubtedly true that the strength of the Renewal or 'Charismatic' movement lay with the Evangelical Charismatics. However their openness to other traditions meant that Church people in these other traditions were reciprocally open to the Evangelicalism of the Evangelical Charismatics. Michael Harper was the leader of the Renewal Movement in the Church of England, but men like David Watson were also very influential.

Evangelical structures and beliefs

There certainly has been and is an Evangelical movement. There are the Anglican Evangelical theological colleges, journals and magazines: the *Church of England Newspaper,* the

Annual Swanwick Conferences (for younger and older Anglican Evangelical clergy); Diocesan Fellowships, the Church of
England Evangelical Council, the central societies like the
Church Pastoral Aid Society with its huge network of youth
organizations in the parishes and its summer camps and, most
important of all, Evangelical publishing — from the *Grove
Booklets* of the indefatigable Colin Buchanan, the new Bishop
of Aston, to heavyweight volumes of biblical scholarship, theology and ethics (some by non-Anglicans, but all identified as
Evangelical).

Unlike the Modern Churchmen's Union the Evangelical focus
is not around ideas but people in the parishes. Evangelism,
worship and social action will motivate Evangelicals. Indeed
they will be as interested as any in serious scholarship and intellectual debate over issues that have a setting in life. But there is
an instinctive impatience with arid academic theology that is
unrelated to the life of faith and practical Christian living.

The typical Evangelical Anglican clergyman of today is
marked by four things at least.

First, he is someone who is a Christian first, an Evangelical
second and an Anglican third.

Second, he is a man who believes that the Bible alone determines matters of faith. But as he reads the Bible he is not
deaf to the traditional interpretation of the Church. Where
Church traditions differ he makes up his own mind; for he
believes that on essential matters, at the end of the day, the
Bible is 'perspicuous' — it is self-evident. And to understand
the Bible it is more important to have a mind open to God than
to have read the latest book. However, interpretation is a work
of the Holy Spirit; he works both in the individual and in the
Church. So he believes that the corporate wisdom of the
Church, as it has been guided by the Holy Spirit, is vital. He is
thus an Evangelical Anglican *Churchman*. And that is why he
takes the Creeds so seriously.

Third, for the Evangelical the Incarnation means unequivo-
cally the deity of Christ. He is usually able to say what current
accounts of the Person of Christ are *incompatible* with the

biblical witness. He often would claim a reverent agnosticism over precisely *how* Jesus is both God and man. It is the same with other problems of Scripture. He can see that certain suggested solutions are incompatible with a living faith in Christ. So he claims here too, when necessary, a reverent agnosticism and prefers to wait for a *Christian* (not a *sub-Christian*) solution.

Fourth, with regard to the issues raised by the Bishop of Durham, he believes Jesus was, of course, born of the Virgin Mary and left the tomb empty in his resurrection. Unlike the Bishop of Durham he does not only want to stress the 'living-ness' of Jesus, but also his 'rising-ness'. As Murray Harris, an Evangelical theologian, has put it:

> After all, in its basic meaning, 'Resurrection' denotes 'restoration to life', not 'life'; a 'rising up' from the tomb and death, not 'being alive again' . . . The Resurrection was basically God's restoration of Jesus to life, not God's perpetuation of the personal impact of Jesus or the disciples' discovery and awareness of his 'livingness'.[7]

What God caused was not a settled conviction among the disciples about Jesus' 'risenness'; 'It was the reanimation and transformation of a buried corpse.'[8]

The twilight generation

This growth of Evangelicalism in the Church of England is among the younger clergy. It is not uniformly experienced across the dioceses. In part this is because the leadership does not reflect this growth, and, in part, that is why the leadership of the Church is going in a different way to many of the clergy and people.

This is not surprising. The impact of what was happening in the student world through Evangelicalism began in the late fifties and the sixties. But a number in the current leadership of the Church were students themselves a little earlier in the forties and early fifties. This was while 'Modernist' teachers were still strong and influential.

But more importantly this was a 'twilight' generation. Christopher Booker has made a study of people who were students in the (late) forties and early fifties — particularly those who were at Oxford and Cambridge. This is where a number of the present bishops were students (at the same time). Christopher Booker says of this generation that it

> was to be placed in a curious position in the years after 1956. On the one hand, they would not be old enough, like their predecessors of the Wilson-Heath generation of the Thirties, to take over the commanding positions of English life. On the other, unlike the post-1956 generation and their non-Oxbridge contemporaries, they were not going to play the leading roles in England's social revolution either. Somehow they were a generation which 'missed out'.[9]

From the secular point of view, this was the generation of Anthony (Tony) Wedgwood Benn, Kenneth Tynan (the critic who wanted the stage and screen to be more 'real', which usually meant more sex and violence), Sir Peter Hall and Lord Snowdon — to name but a few.

This generation supported radical change. The Second World War had negatively stopped Hitler, but positively it had achieved little. There was no bright new vision and the austerity of the late forties seemed rather drab. So this generation were prepared to try something different. They were iconoclasts. They acted as brokers for the new permissiveness. They enabled the Beatles, the Rolling Stones, drugs and the pill (and David Frost) to change our whole culture in the sixties. But they acted more as midwives: they were the editors, the photographers, the promoters and the producers of others.

The secular (non-clerical) members of this generation reached positions of influence in the world far sooner than their clerical contemporaries have reached positions of influence in the Church. It was in the sixties that they came into their own. Indeed they were the architects of the swinging sixties, bringing about considerable cultural change. Yet all this is a thing of the past now: the ideas of that generation are no longer relevant. Vietnam and Third World issues have affected everyone. And the world is taking leadership more and more from those born in the thirties, not in the twenties (look at the birth dates of many key politicians).

A last fling

In the Church, however, this generation has now reached the traditional age for episcopal leadership. It is interesting to see how some among this generation of leaders are trying to influence the Church: some of them, the doubting bishops, appear to be acting as their secular contemporaries did in the sixties!

It would, of course, be very wrong to press too far this observation on the 'age' of the current leadership. But it at least raises some questions and suggests some possible answers.

The sixties may have been a last fling of humanistic excess, while the hopes of a world enlightened by human effort were fading. So some in the current leadership in the Church of England may be representing a last fling of a Church worn out by liberal Protestantism. The very serious question is 'Will the liberal leadership destroy the Church in the process?'

Of course, there is a resonance among a number of the clergy for the views of these 'doubting bishops'. These will be older Modernists and the younger clergy who came into the ministry influenced by the *Honest to God* generation (the swinging theological sixties), and others more recently who have been influenced by the recent extreme Radicalism. And sadly there will be those that have experienced that theological brainwashing we earlier referred to. Over this period, particularly in the late sixties and early seventies, Evangelicals had to spend their energies 'getting back into the Church' and focusing more on ecclesiological questions. They had neither the time nor yet the strength to take on the new Radicalism. That was left to their Anglo-Catholic brethren, with men such as E. L. Mascall. But the Anglo-Catholic cause was beginning to decline, and this was not a strong counter. Hence the current relative strength of those ready to give a listening ear to the Bishop of Durham.

But none of this should blind the current leadership to what is really happening in the Church, the Nation and the world. Change is happening. An era going back more than two hundred years is coming to an end!

So the bishops of the Church need to have a wider view. For in a voluntary, non-profit organization like the Church it is very difficult to try to lead where other people have already *consciously* decided they are not going.

Some of the current bishops and theologians were chaplains or deans at Oxbridge Colleges during the period which saw the beginnings of Evangelical growth. But this growth in itself meant a rejection of the Modernist liberal Protestantism that some of these bishops and theologians, as younger men, stood for. These Modernist chaplains and deans usually interpreted this rejection as 'mindless fundamentalism'. This in itself hardened the Evangelical students in their rejection of Modernist theology all the more. For they argued like this: 'If these men make such bad judgements about what we know first hand, the chances are they are making bad judgements elsewhere!'

But there is one other problem with the leadership of the Church we must note, for it affects theology. The Church is often at the mercy of secular institutions for its theological leadership and, therefore, for some of its bishops! Some of the 'doubting bishops', along with some of our 'doubting theologians', got their first recognition through Oxbridge Colleges where they were chaplains or deans. In those positions they *taught* a number of the next generation of ordinands and clergy. But they were usually appointed not by the Church but by the governing body of their respective colleges — the other Fellows. However, many of these are overtly non-Christian! At one Oxford College, not so long ago, a well-known Marxist was the senior member of an appointing group.

The appointment of bishops

But who appoints a man a bishop? In July 1974 the General Synod decided that the Church of England itself should have more of a say in the appointment of bishops. Up to that time the Prime Minister appointed bishops — when a vacancy occurred, the Prime Minister submitted names to the Crown (the Sovereign is seen as the senior 'administrator' of the

Church of England). True, Sir John Hewitt, the Prime Minister's Appointments Secretary, in the sixties had developed a consultative procedure. But it was all very secret. And the Church didn't like the system.

So in 1974 the then Archbishop of Canterbury and Sir Norman Anderson, the Chairman of the House of Laity, had discussions with the Prime Minister and Parliamentary leaders. The result was an agreement that the General Synod would appoint a small committee to assess a vacancy and decide on two names, which could be put in order of preference. These would be given to the Prime Minister who would retain the right to recommend the second name or to ask the committee for a further name or names.

This has been the system since 1977 for appointing bishops. The committee, called the Crown Appointments Commission, consists of twelve members. These are the two Archbishops, three members elected from the clergy of the General Synod, three elected from the laity of the General Synod, plus four members appointed by the vacancy-in-see committee of the diocese where there is a vacancy.

But is it right that a prime minister, who might have only loose connections with the Church, should appoint its senior leaders? Why should not the Crown Appointments Commission submit one name directly to the Queen? The constitutional monarchy in the United Kingdom means that the Sovereign acts on the advice of her ministers. But an adjustment in the appointment of bishops is hardly a threat to constitutional monarchy! Nor is it a threat to the Sovereign's prerogative. A name could always be rejected, in the same way as the Archbishop always has the right not to consecrate the Crown's nominee.

However, even with the ideal structure it would not necessarily be easy to fill bishoprics. According to a report in *The Times* (March 28th 1984):

The Church of England is apparently having increasing difficulty filling its top positions with the men it wants. It has become acceptable, with no loss of face or reprimand, for an archdeacon, dean, suffragan bishop or theology professor to decline an invitation to fill a vacant See, and as a result some senior positions have been filled by the church's second — or third or fourth — choice . . . It is widely known that the present Archbishop of Canterbury, Dr Robert Runcie, turned down the offer of the Archbishopric of York when he was Bishop of St Alban's.

The Bishop of Southwark then wrote in to say the problem could well be one's children: 'some of them may still be at school. The timing of any move . . . can become an acutely difficult decision.'

But apart from an individual's personal reluctance to move, there is the serious problem of finding a suitable candidate for a Church which has ever-widening doctrinal boundaries. If every doctrinal eccentricity is to be tolerated within the Church, only those men of a very liberal or an indefinite turn of mind will be able to be bishops. For it is only such men who are capable of thinking (wrongly) that all doctrines point to the truth. In a weak sense they alone can oversee (exercise *episcope* in respect of) everybody. But the man who believes certain views to be definitely wrong, whether he be Anglo-Catholic or Evangelical will be less suitable. There is thus an institutional bias in a Church which does not exercise doctrinal discipline towards appointing theologically liberal leaders.

In addition many think that there is an institutional bias towards surrounding bishops with a liberal bureaucracy and staff; and this reinforces the liberal leadership. For as church growth and theologically liberal ideas are incompatible, Radical or Modernist clergy are likely to find it depressing in parish life with ever-dwindling congregations. However they can retreat from these hard realities by going into Diocesan or General Synod jobs (or into theological teaching or broadcasting).

But some of a definite persuasion will be chosen. Thank God, there are always exceptions to every rule — or bias.

PART 3

Practical Problems and Possibilities

12

Leadership for growth — basic perspectives

The Church of England — where is it going? It is now time to move from analysis to some suggested ways forward. We have spoken about the Church of England and where it now stands. We must now say where it ought to be going. There are, as we have seen, great problems in the Church of England. But, under God, it has potentially a great future. However, certain things need to be recognized and certain other things need to happen. We must now spend time discussing these. Having been theoretical, we must now try to be practical. And having focused on bishops we must now focus on the practical problems of the parochial clergy as well.

First, we must understand that there are preconditions for the Church of England's health — nationally and parochially. As we said earlier, there are four essential factors, and all four have to be working together. These are: one, agreed goals; two, competent leadership; three, enabling structures; and, four, an awareness of and interaction with the social environment. These are four essentials necessary for any organization's health, but especially for the health of the Church.

We have so far been focusing on doctrinal issues and beliefs as they affect the life of the Church. And this is all in the area of the 'agreed goals' of the Church; for the Church's goals spring from its fundamental beliefs. And we have already suggested that high up among the current goals must be the growth of the Church.

But 'agreed goals' are only one element in the Church's life. This is the first and most vital element. But it is not all. The Church of England could be as orthodox and clearheaded as one could wish with regard to the Virgin Birth and the Empty Tomb, but that by itself would get us nowhere. In James' Epistle it is said that 'the demons believe'! 'Belief' is necessary, but not sufficient. It is necessary, because the Church will never have 'agreed goals' if there is fundamental disagreement over belief. But it is not sufficient; sadly there are many theologically orthodox churches that are dead.

The Church also needs 'competent leadership' for its goals to be translated into action. So it needs to be working at its leadership and its understanding of leadership. We have begun to see this in the last chapter. But leadership in the Church is more than the selection of bishops! If the Church is to move forward, it must move forward in every aspect of leadership. There need to be new attitudes, a new understanding and a new learning of leadership skills.

Managing

Senior leadership in the Church is exercised by the bishops and clergy. In the Reformed tradition within which the Church of England stands this leadership is traditionally understood in two ways — it is understood on the one hand as a *prophetic* leadership and on the other hand it is understood as a *priestly* leadership.

The 'prophetic' role of the bishops and clergy is exercised through the ministry of the word — through preaching and teaching. That ministry is both directed to those outside and inside the Church. It involves the ministry of the word to the local and the national community (this is where the bishops sitting in the House of Lords have a special opportunity and responsibility). It, of course, also means the ministry of the word in the local Church and congregation.

The 'priestly' role of the bishops and clergy is exercised through pastoral work and the ministry of the sacraments.

Evangelicals would put greater stress on pastoral work, Anglo-Catholics on the ministry of the sacraments.

And this is the self-understanding of the majority of those in positions of ordained leadership in the Church of England to-day. They see themselves as 'prophets' and/or 'priests'. However, there is clearly something missing! Let me explain.

The leader functions 'in the name of Jesus Christ'. In the Gospel account Jesus said to 'the seventy' he appointed: 'He who hears you hears me' (Lk 10:16). This seems to show that the leader or Christian worker represents Christ to some extent.

But Jesus Christ was not only our Prophet and Priest, but also our King (as John Newton's hymn so elegantly reminds us). And, when we think about it, there is obviously a 'kingly' role as well as a 'prophetic' and 'priestly' role that the Christian leader has to exercise. He has to 'rule'; he has to 'manage'; he has to exercise 'oversight' or, using the transliteration of the Greek word, he has to exercise *episcope*.

We certainly have to be careful. Any kingly (ruling) aspect of Christian leadership has to be Christ-like. Jesus Christ indeed ruled and lead; and he was strong in his rule and leadership. But he did not exercise this kingly ministry as the Gentiles did. He was the king on a donkey! He exercised his rule not by domination but by service. 'Whoever would be great among you must be your servant, and whoever would be first among you must be slave of all [not, notice, slave of *some*; to serve *all* often you have to oppose *some*!]' (Mk 10:43-44). This does not mean non-leadership or non-rule. It means the leader has to achieve his goals not by force but by motivation through loving service.

The rural model of ministry

But management, or the art of ruling, in a Christ-like way is not automatic. Indeed at the moment we have a crisis of leadership in the Church. On the one hand there is some evidence that the current doctrinal confusion is deterring some young men (and women) from entering full-time service in the Church of England. This is serious; for if the stock of future leaders begins to dry up, the future itself is jeopardized. But on the other hand we are in a situation where many in positions of leadership are finding the task very hard. This is not through any fault of their own, but through a combination of circumstances.

First, and perhaps the most serious problem is what we can call 'the problem of the rural model' of ministry. For centuries the majority of the clergy of the Church of England ministered in what we might call rural situations. The typical (and so idealized) social form of the parish became that of a small community of only several hundred to a thousand parishioners. Even in small market towns, the basic shape was not very different: it was an immobile community, with people living and working on the spot. The model parish was therefore one where one man ministered as chaplain to this community. Of course there were many variations on this theme (and the clergyman who did most of the work might have been a curate of an absentee vicar). Indeed, only in the second half of the nineteenth century did England even come near to achieving the goal of 'one man one parish'. But be that as it may, the following is certain: there has been impressed on the consciousness of the Church of England a style of parochial working that we can fairly call 'rural'. It is not for nothing that Newcastle Central Deanery, in the heartland of the industrial North-East, still has a 'Rural Dean'!

But what is this style like? It is a style appropriate to a rural or pre-industrial situation. It is appropriate for a small Church with a *congregation* of up to 150 worshippers (just what you might expect where there is a 'good' man in a large village or small market town). In such a situation the clergyman sees his job as 'study' in the morning (after he has prayed — in a cold church if he is an Anglo-Catholic, in a warm vicarage if he is an Evangelical). In the afternoon he would do some visiting. Before tea he would make sure any necessary odd jobs were done in the vicarage garden or the churchyard. After tea he would go out to a committee meeting, or perhaps to a dinner with some more well-to-do parishioners. On Saturday he would occasionally take weddings. On Sundays he would take services. And when (sadly) it was required, he would bury the dead.

Now for this job you need basically to be a person-orientated parson. It is a 'pastoral' job in the conventional sense of that word (i.e. a caring job — that is what the afternoon visiting is all about). *Little management is required at all.* One man can function perfectly well 'flying by the seat of his pants'. Personableness, compassion, manners, a reasonable intelligence and wit (as a bonus) are all that is needed, in terms of human qualities. This, then, becomes (and it has become) the 'model' of the clergyman.

Selection for ministry

Therefore, young men when they are considering the ministry have this as the understanding of what they may be involved in later. The more person-orientated man will be attracted. The more task-orientated man assumes the ministry is not for him. And this is very serious, *for it is such task-orientated men who are more likely to be able to lead growing churches,* as we shall be seeing!

But the grip of this rural model of ministry means that the Church is paralysed to a large extent. For a church is unlikely to grow beyond 150 unless it is led by a man with church management skills and who is more task-orientated. This is because once a congregation at worship exceeds 150 you have a management situation. The senior leadership in such a church, therefore, has to be able to manage. That is something very different from being good at pastoral work.

However, this rural model is the one usually held out to prospective ordinands if they are thinking about parochial ministry. So the clergyman who 'does it all' in the parish cannot be said to be guilty. His motivation for entering the ministry was to care for people by sharing with them the gospel of Jesus Christ, and he believed he was called to do that sharing. He was encouraged in this by the Advisory Council for the Church's Ministry (or its predecessor), the body responsible for the selection and training of men for the ordained ministry in the Church of England. His gifts are probably along these pastoral lines.

But we need in the Church of England a radical shift of perspective if we are to have growth. Of course, there still will be the need, in a subordinate place, for the old rural model. But by itself that will not lead to the growth of existing churches, as we shall see.

In the light of all this, it is a sobering fact to realize that three-quarters of all Anglican churches have under 100 at worship — according to the statistics of the Nationwide Initiative in Evangelism survey of 1979. The survey also gave figures for Protestant Church attendance as a whole. Of the 39,000 churches the Sunday attendance figures indicated that there were very few with over 500; less than 1 per cent had 301–500; 6 per cent had 151–300; 56 per cent had 26–150; and 37 per cent had under 25. But this is no way to minister to the nation. As most of the population is now in urban areas, you must have churches that can minister appropriately in urban contexts. They must provide a range of ministries appropriate to modern urban needs. Small churches find that very hard. For example you cannot run effective Christian youth programmes with only a handful of children whose ages range from 1 to 18! But unless the leadership of the Church is trained for growth and can *manage growth*, the majority of churches will remain under 150 strong.

The need for training

Another factor that inhibits growth is that some in the highest positions of leadership in the Church of England have themselves had very little experience of church growth or even ordinary parish life. Some of the current bishops have done one curacy and then gone back to university work or theological college teaching. From there, after perhaps a *short* parochial charge, they are asked to become bishops (but it often takes six years properly to understand a church and to shape it for growth).

Of course, theological expertise is important; but we mustn't confuse theological expertise with 'leadership'. Indeed, had the bishops over recent years properly understood leadership, the dynamics of parochial life and what makes churches grow, it is unthinkable that they would have allowed the Church of England to drift into the current state of doctrinal confusion. The conclusion being drawn (rightly or wrongly) is that some of them simply don't understand parochial life.

Nor is this to 'blame' any individual bishop. We do not blame our 'model' parish clergyman who finds it difficult to enable a church to grow above 150. Nor must we blame a bishop who has neither had much experience of parish life *from the inside* nor the experience of church growth. If he doesn't understand what helps a parish move forward and if he finds it difficult to encourage clergy for growth and to structure the diocese for growth, that is not his fault. But blame will be incurred if these facts are not faced. There will be blame, too, not just on individuals, but on the Church at large if it doesn't face the problem.

The solution is all-round training for growth. We will be discussing aspects of church growth later. But leadership training needs to be underlined on its own. It is so important. Indeed, the North-East Clergy's *Position* (see Appendix 1) came to the following conclusion:

> That new initiatives should be taken to help the clergy of the North-East in personal holiness, their ministry of teaching, preaching, worship, *and also the practice of church growth, management and leadership;* also that more ordinands and full-time workers should be recruited and trained.

The first steps to implementation of that proposal came with the setting-up of a modest *North East Programme for Ministry* in February 1985. One session of this programme was devoted to 'leadership for growth'.

There is much that can be taught. And the Americans have

much to teach us. We need to be humble enough to learn from them. Seminaries like Fuller Theological Seminary in Pasadena run a 'Continuing Education Programme' for clergy. This is leadership training with an emphasis on growth.

Five cost factors

Peter Wagner is Professor of Church Growth at Fuller and has recently written *Leading Your Church to Growth*. A popular book, there is much good material in it. It reminds us that if the Church of England is to see growth, there is a price that its leadership will have to pay. Only a part of what Peter Wagner says can be summarized here.

Peter Wagner points out that leadership for growth is costly, and some leaders (bishops and clergy) may simply not be prepared for the costs. But what are these costs? He identifies five cost factors.

First, there is the cost of *assuming the responsibility for growth*. Some clergy are not willing to begin to think of growth. Perhaps this is because there is the risk of failure — and the fear of failure is a great barrier to some men. Then, so many men have never been trained for growing churches at theological college. There are yet others who are not sure of God's call to the particular work they are in. So why bother to help it grow?

John Wimber surveyed churches with over 200 at worship and growing at 100 per cent per decade. These were two of the findings: all the clergy knew that God had called them originally into the ministry; and all the clergy knew absolutely they were called to their current places of ministry!

Second, there is the cost of *working hard*. Peter Wagner writes:

> The church growth pastors I know are putting in long hours in planning, meeting with people who influence the growth process in one way or another, in prayer and the seeking of God's leading, in study and research, in putting out fires, but most of all in dreaming God's dreams after Him. And all this on top of the routine duties of being a pastor.[1]

A study has been undertaken of ten of the largest churches in the Assemblies of God in America. The report indicated that the pastors of all ten churches had considerable leadership gifts. Then it said: 'A common denominator of all these pastors . . . is their strong work habits. They are not lazy men, but work hard. Their churches reflect their efforts.'[2]

Part of working hard, of course, involves learning about church growth. That is not easy when a bishop or clergyman is already very busy. But it means visiting and studying growing churches, reading literature on church growth and attending courses and seminars, such as those put on at Fuller or some of the courses now offered in this country.

Third, there is the cost of *sharing the ministry*. If a church is to grow above 150 this is essential. The ministry will have to be shared with other full-time staff and with lay members of the congregation. One man simply has not the necessary time and energy to minister adequately once the church begins to grow above 150. He cannot then do all the preaching, teaching, counselling, visiting, training, nurturing, administration, evangelism and maintain good community relations.

So once a church gets to this size it will have to add one more full-time staff person. But for the 'loner', having to work with someone else is sometimes quite costly. There will also have to be delegation — and some find that very difficult.

Fourth, there is the cost of *having members you can't pastor*. This again is related to our rural model of the parochial clergyman. Such a man has what Peter Wagner calls 'the heart of a pastor or a shepherd':

> You have a need to know the names of all your church members and their families, visit each home *x* number of times per year, make an extra call or two to everyone who is sick, do all the counselling, perform all the baptisms, weddings and funerals, lend a hand in personal problems, and enjoy a type of family relationship with one and all.[3]

But if the church is to grow, the clergyman has to move from a *shepherd* role to that of a *farm manager*. The sheep will still be shepherded, but the farm manager does not do everything. He sees that it is done by others. But the trouble is that person-orientated clergy often have a 'person need' and are unwilling or unable to pay this particular price of leadership for growth.

Fifth, there is the cost of *revising non-growth theology*. It isn't just forms of modernistic theology that will have to be given up. There are many 'orthodox' clergy who have little concern for growth. They often say they have been called to be 'faithful' not 'successful'. Peter Wagner refers to the parable of the talents in Jesus' teaching (Mt 25:14-30). The *faithful* servants were the ones who had made some money and were *successful*. They were faithful in that they were having a measure of success:

> They were faithful because they were successful in taking the master's resources and using them for the master's purpose. The un-faithful servant did not accomplish the master's goal, or in other words he was unsuccessful.[4]

Nor can we in England dismiss this as the American obsession with success. This line of arguing is no different from the philosophy of ministry adopted by Richard Baxter (1615-91), a Puritan and author of the classic, *The Reformed Pastor*. In it he wrote these words:

> Moreover, if you would prosper in your work, be sure to keep up earnest desires and expectations of success. If your hearts be not set on the end of your labours, and you long not to see the conversion and edification of your hearers, and do not study and preach in hope, you are not likely to see much fruit of it . . . I know that a faithful minister may have comfort when he wants success; and our acceptance is not according to the fruit, but according to our labour: but then, he that longeth not for the success of his labours can have none of this comfort, because he was not a faithful labourer . . . For it is not only our own reward that we labour for, but other men's salvation. I confess, for my part, I marvel at some ancient, reverend men that have lived twenty or forty or fifty years with an unprofitable people, among whom they have seen little fruit of their labours that it was scarce discernible how they can, with so much patience, there go on. Were it my case, though I durst not leave the vineyard, nor quit my calling, yet I should suspect that it was God's will I should go somewhere else, and another come in my place that might be fitter for them. And I should not be easily satisfied to spend my days in such a sort.[5]

13

Leadership for growth — simple essentials

The New Testament makes it quite clear that training for leadership should be a priority. Three of the New Testament Epistles are pastoral Epistles — letters written to men in positions of leadership in the Church, to encourage them in their work. And in the Church of England, if it is to reverse its decline, strengthening leadership must be a top priority.

It is noticeable that in the New Testament the spiritual life of the leader and his character are highlighted. A leader in the Church, we are told, has to be:

> above reproach, the husband of but one wife, temperate, self-controlled, respectable, hospitable, able to teach, and not given to much wine, not violent but gentle, not quarrelsome, not a lover of money. He must manage his own family well and see that his children obey him with proper respect. (If anyone does not know how to manage his own family, how can he take care of God's church?) He must not be a recent convert, or he may become conceited and fall under the same judgement as the devil. He must also have a good reputation with outsiders, so that he will not fall into disgrace and into the devil's trap (1 Tim 3:2-7 New International Version).

His job is there described as 'taking care of God's Church'. That is to say, he is to manage it in a loving way. But his personal character is all important, as is his moral behaviour and his home life.

Prayer

It is fair to say, therefore, that renewal of Church leadership has to begin in the leader's personal and private life. And that will surely mean revitalizing, in the first place, the prayer life of our bishops and clergy.

One of the most impressive things about Paul Yonggi Cho, the Pentecostal Pastor of the huge Full Gospel Central Church, in Seoul, Korea, is the emphasis he puts on prayer. He spends a great deal of time in prayer himself and he teaches the church regularly about prayer. He writes:

> One of the greatest lies of Satan is that we just don't have enough time to pray. However, all of us have enough time to sleep, eat and breathe. As soon as we realize that prayer is as important as sleeping, eating and breathing, we will be amazed at how much more time will be available to us for prayer.[1]

The Full Gospel Central Church has its own Prayer Mountain — a retreat a few miles outside Seoul. At the weekend thousands make use of it, and many use it during the week also

If God is responsible for the growth of his Church, it is essential that we pray. We will not be able to achieve our goals without his aid. But the example in prayer must be set by the leadership.

A leader can devise programmes, preach well, build new buildings and raise money on his own. Such is the desperate need for human community in today's impersonal world that by native wit he may be able to attract a large number of people. But no deep and lasting spiritual work will be done. For such a work, the Holy Spirit must bring men and women to a conviction of their needs and then bring them to new life in Christ. This seems to be the teaching of the New Testament. However, Jesus taught that the Holy Spirit is given in answer to prayer.

Ron Jenson and Jim Stevens sum it up like this:

> The church was not designed to run with man at the controls. If the church is to grow it must be dependent on God. If it is dependent, it will also be expectant. The whole process will become the

great adventure it was meant to be: the adventure of seeing the living God regularly doing things that cannot be explained in human terms. If we know that only God can make things happen, then we will ask Him for the impossible and believe that He will do it.[2]

Prayer and faith will always go together. As leaders in the church have a growing vision of God and what he can do, so they will be motivated to pray. When they pray and begin to see things happening in answer to prayer, faith will increase and there will be more prayer. It is the biblical principle of 'to him that hath it shall be given'!

Prayer and faith cannot, however, be nurtured in a climate of unbelief. Such a climate is being caused by those bishops who seem today to doubt the significance of petitionary prayer and who seem to make the whole exercise so complicated. Professor E. M. Blaiklock has some wise words on this:

> The Lord was never more simple than when he taught men to pray. There are those who turn prayer into an exercise in resignation, a form of quietism, a ritual of meditation, or a process of psychological therapy. If Christ is to be heard on the theme, prayer is simply speaking to 'our Father in Heaven' . . . A father yearns for some interchange of love from his children, he treasures their complete confidence, he listens with sympathy to their smallest requests: although in his wider wisdom he does not always grant them, he is never deaf to their appeals, unmoved by their fears, or untouched by their anxieties, even though he may know that the appeals are unwise, the fears without foundation, and the anxieties groundless.[3]

Self-organization

Timothy, a New Testament leader, was told: 'Take heed to yourself' (1 Tim 4:16). Every leader at some point has to come to grips with his own time management and self-organization. And the Church of England is unlikely to grow unless its clergy learn this art.

In his *Book of Isaiah* Sir George Adam Smith calls attention to the word *judgement* or *justice* in Isaiah 30:18: 'The Lord is a God of justice (judgement)'. And *judgement* means here, he says, 'method, design, order, system, law'. So God is a God of method and order. Therefore, he requires of those whom he trusts with leadership that 'all things be done decently and in order.' 'It is a great truth,' writes Smith, 'that the All-mighty and All-merciful is the *All-methodical* too; and no religion is complete in its creed, or healthy in its influence, which does not insist equally on all these.'[4]

Let me make four preliminary points about this subject of self-organization.

First, we have to distinguish efficiency from effectiveness. Efficiency is doing the job right and effectiveness is doing the right job. Too many of us get caught up in efficiency. The goal of self-organization is to make sure we are effective — doing the right job. And as we have said, that must mean we are contributing to the growth of the Church.

Secondly, we must realize that there is no way we will be able to organize others if we don't organize ourselves first. And the number one essential in self-organization is to *plan our time*. We must make sure that the precious twenty-four hours we have in the day are spent on the *right* activities. These are the ones that will make us effective and help us achieve what we are in our jobs to do. Unfortunately so many Christian leaders get sidetracked with doing apparently worthwhile activities, but which in no way make them effective or help contribute to the growth of the Church or the extension of God's kingdom!

Thirdly, we have to ask the basic question of ourselves: 'What am I here for (in my job — as a bishop, an archdeacon, a vicar, a layman etc.)?' And this is why it is essential we do not have doctrinal confusion in the Church. If we are at 'sixes and sevens' theologically, we will not be able to answer that primary question. And that is probably why a number of the clergy are today frustrated and depressed. They have not got a clear idea of what their ministry goals are to be.

The simple answer to this question is that a leader (a bishop, a clergyman, a Sunday School superintendent etc) is to help the Church achieve its goals. But we can only agree on goals as a Church, when we are agreed about fundamental beliefs. So today, almost contradictory answers about goals may be given. With radically different answers being given, the wider organization of the Church of England is continually being frustrated. Nor will it ever be able to function correctly until there is significantly more doctrinal agreement than there is at present.

Fourthly, we have to see that *how long* we spend on any given job depends on how important it is. *How soon* a job has to be done depends on how urgent it is. And as has been well said: 'The "important" is seldom "urgent" and the "urgent" is often not "important".' But how do we decide what is important?

The watch and the diary

Many would argue that in determining what is important we must distinguish between positive *pro-active* tasks from the more *re-active* tasks.

What are 're-active' tasks? The 're-active' tasks are all the things that come our way as we react to the existing situation. Most of the phone calls and letters we have to deal with, many of the problems we have to face daily, are re-active. A friend of mine asked a bishop once what was his goal for the diocese. His reply: 'I just want to clear my desk by each evening.' At least he was honest! He was simply re-acting.

Tina Tietjen says:

> The danger, and this is the trap most unorganised managers are caught up in, is that you will spend all the available time on reactive tasks — coping with the day-to-day jobs — and no time, or very little time, on the positive tasks.[5]

By contrast, the positive pro-active tasks are the ones that help us achieve the goals of our ministry — all the things that will help the Church move forward. So these include all the tasks and activities that contribute towards the growth of the Church. They may be very menial or they may be very exciting.

Naturally *it is the positive pro-active tasks that are impor-*

tant. The re-active tasks are less important (unless, of course, they are pastoral emergencies). They are *necessary,* but we should try and get through them as quickly as possible, and where possible we should try to delegate. It goes without saying that anything that is *both* important *and* urgent is an absolute priority.

From time to time it is, therefore, essential to sit down with a sheet of paper and to classify the work we do — all the activities that go to make up our days. Then we must distinguish between what is pro-active from what is re-active and distinguish between what is urgent from what is non-urgent.

We can then begin to set priorities. And we *must* set them. For when we list out our work something will happen. We will see exactly *how* it is that we have been so hard pressed for time and *how* it is that we have far too much to do. Often we don't realize this until we write things down.

So we must then get out our diaries and schedule our time and set our priorities in the light of what is important and what is urgent. The clergyman who said that the two most important things in his ministry were his watch and his diary, may have been criticized by the 'super-spiritual', but he had a point.

The first requirement in marking up a diary is to set time or diary space for important pro-active tasks. This will include time for planning on our own, and being able to stand back from the re-active tasks and the situation as it is, and praying and thinking about where God wants us (our group, our church, our diocese) to be. We then allow time or diary space for re-active tasks; and unless they are pastoral emergencies, we aim to get through these as quickly as possible.

Delegation

If you analyse your work in the suggested way, many of the tasks you do will be found to be unimportant. You will realize that a number can and should be delegated.

Delegation is a very sophisticated art, however. It certainly *doesn't* mean just asking someone to do a job, and then letting him or her get on with it. This is not delegation but the creation of a new task. Also some Church leaders confuse delegation with co-ordination. Leadership will involve both, but in delegation part of your leadership is delegated. It is assigning to someone else part of *your* job and responsibility. Therefore, of course, you can't just off-load onto someone else part of *your* job unless at the same time you make sure they can off-load onto someone else part of *their* job or they have time to spare.

First, you have to decide what aspect of your own work you are wanting to delegate and to whom you are intending to delegate it. Then you have to brief and, if necessary, train the person you are delegating your work to. And briefing needs to be quite specific. It includes what is delegated as well as what is *not* delegated. It also includes establishing levels of authority. 'Perhaps more confusion is created here than in any other aspect of delegation', writes Ted Engstrom.[6]

There are two basic levels of authority in delegation. First, 'act and report'. Here the individual concerned takes initiative and acts, but afterwards reports back to his leader, either regularly, periodically or immediately. But the second level is where a person acts after approval. In this case there first will be consultation. Both are legitimate. It simply depends on the nature of the work delegated. The vital thing is that everybody knows what is expected from the outset.

It is also important when delegating that you tell others what is going on. For if they expect you still to be responsible and suddenly find someone else has taken over, that is very annoying.

But after the new system is working you must continue to be available for help when required. John Stott once admitted he had to learn this lesson:

> I myself have only recently learned that the true art of delegation is not to hand over work to somebody else and then forget all about it, but to commit work to a deputy who knows that he is responsible to you and can at times report back and seek advice.[7]

Last, you have to build in check-points when you review the work that has been delegated. This is for comparing notes and quite unashamedly checking on progress.

Problems in delegation

You can't always delegate, however. Here are four examples. First, you cannot delegate policy-making if that is yours to oversee. Second, you cannot delegate, if you are the only person who knows how to do the job. You first must engage in extensive training of someone else. Third, you cannot delegate responsibility for the people who are *immediately* under you. Fourth, you cannot (or should not) delegate simply to 'pass the buck'.

What are the pitfalls in delegation? As we have said, people can assume that they have more authority than has been given them, and people fail to report back in consequence. There is also the difficult and fine balance between being interfering but yet not waiting until disaster occurs before doing anything. Ted Engstrom says:

> There is a fine line between 'back-seat driving' and stepping in when it is necessary: use your best judgement to avoid the one, yet be ready to do the other.[8]

At our Church in Jesmond we make use of the *Video Arts* management training films,[9] which feature the inimitable John Cleese. In a very humorous way, they fulfil a number of training needs. Made for the commercial world, they have much that is relevant to the Church and church growth. The films in the series that go to make up *The Unorganised Manager* are a 'must' for everyone who wants to take St Paul's words seriously about self-organization! Some of the points outlined above are brilliantly dealt with in these films.

Extending the leadership

What has been said about delegation is relevant for an arch-bishop, a bishop, a vicar, a curate, a Sunday School superintendent, a co-ordinator of home groups — anyone in fact. The principles refer to any leadership, whether leadership is ordained or lay, employed (full-time) or voluntary. Indeed, in the Church most of the leadership will be lay and voluntary. But as the lay leadership evolves, so there will be need of more full-time leadership to co-ordinate this new leadership.

If the Church is to grow, growth in leadership is essential. David Womack makes the point in *The Pyramid Principle*: 'Before a church may add to its mass of members and adherents, it must expand its base of organization and ministry (leadership).'[10] Jenson and Stevens write:

> This is like piling sand on a table. You can pile on only so much sand before the table is covered. When you have no more space the sand starts flowing onto the floor. If you want and need to hold more sand, you must enlarge the table. That is the point of the pyramid principle: add to the base and then you can expand the operation. Increase qualified leadership (and organizational structure) and then your church may grow, both qualitatively and quantitatively.[11]

But increasing full-time workers is not always so easy. Nor is money the main problem. For a good new staff person will enable the church to grow more; and the increase in activity and numbers through new converts pays for their salary within two years. The problem is finding the right person!

Increasing voluntary workers is almost as difficult. We always think that problems over the recruitment of volunteers are 'peculiar to our situations'. Other churches, we think, find it easy. Middle-class churches think that the problem is that their people are too busy holding down responsible jobs. Working-class churches think that their people aren't always gifted enough. But identifying gifts, recruiting and training volunteers is never easy. It has to be a *major task* for someone in the church's leadership. For the process of involving the lay person in ministry or in leadership is a very demanding activity.

First, we are back to the voluntary, non-profit status of the Church. The layman in the Church cannot be forced or threatened in the way the Government (a 'non-voluntary, non-profit organization) can force and threaten people through the courts. Nor can he be forced or threatened in the way a business company (a 'voluntary, for profit' organization) uses the force or threats of financial sanctions. In the local church the layman simply votes with his feet and opts out if he so decides. That is why motivation and expectations are so important in the Church.

Secondly, there is an added difficulty found especially in the more Evangelical churches. This is the Protestant spirit. Here the individual may be confident of a 'hot line' to God. Such a lay person (the Sunday School teacher, creche worker, home-group member, those doing practical jobs etc) is convinced he or she is working exclusively for 'the Lord'. Thus if the Sunday School leader delegates to the Sunday School teacher a certain job, the teacher can fail to see that he or she has a responsibility *to their leader* as well as 'to the Lord'. They think that they are *only* answerable to the Lord! So if they want to do the job totally differently, they can easily tell themselves 'it is the Lord's will!' And that is the way they wi! do it. Problems usually follow.

As a rule, leaders in the church do have to be obeyed, because as Hebrews puts it: 'Your leaders . . . are keeping watch over your souls, as men who will have to give account' (13:17). If the issue seems important, the 'subordinate' should try to persuade the 'superior' of their differing point of view. If they succeed, well and good. If they fail, that is that. They have to do what they were asked to do; or if to them it is a serious matter of conscience, they have to resign. What they should not do is to continue doing the job in their own way against the instructions of their own leader (be it the Sunday School Superintendent or anyone else). To do so is 'the Judges Syndrome': 'In those days there was no king in Israel; every man did what was right in his own eyes' (Judg 21:25).

Problems in lay leadership

There are other hurdles that have to be overcome in effective lay working and in securing lay leadership. One is the fact that quite often potential leaders in the church are under pressure of some sort. The clergyman was not unique who said, when talking about lay leadership: 'Almost everyone I've got in a position of leadership is going through some kind of personal crisis. They can't take leadership because it is all they can do to contend with their own lives.'

This is an experience shared by many clergy. But J. D. Anderson and E. E. Jones speak of church groups 'that not only accomplished their tasks but became for the members a primary source of healing and support during a critical life passage.'[12] It is important, therefore, to realize that continuing involvement may be helpful. And so the wise pastor sometimes should not agree to release people too soon from leadership roles — not for the church's sake but for their own sakes. Clearly, judgement is required.

Another hurdle to overcome is finding people with the right qualifications. Leaders need to have biblical qualifications. After all, it is God's call that the local church is wanting to discover — even in humble duties. Lay leaders, certainly if they are sharing in the ministry of the word, will need to be spiritually mature and measure up to the biblical qualifications for that sort of leadership. If we follow the principle of the appointment of 'the seven' in Acts 6 we will want even those involved in finance to be men or women 'full of the Spirit and of wisdom'. The budget (or the specific financial target) is perhaps the most significant theological statement the parish puts out during the year. It reflects what that church believes is God's will: where the church believes it should be going; and what the church believes people should be challenged about.

Finally, many would say there are four essential characteristics the lay leader should show: regular attendance; faithfulness and loyalty to the philosophy of the church, the vicar and the other leaders; willingness to do the job; and, obviously, capability.

14

Enabling structures?

The Church of England is quite clear as to what a church is. It is certainly not a building. Rather it is people. This is how it is put in the Thirty-nine Articles:

> The visible Church of Christ is a congregation of faithful men, in the which the pure Word of God is preached, and the Sacraments be duly ministered according to Christ's ordinance in all those things that of necessity are requisite to the same (Article XIX *Of the Church*).

The parish church

This means that the 'local church' is not the diocese, or the deanery, it is *the parish*. At the heart of the Church of England is the parish church. And it is the people who gather together for worship, to hear God's word and partake of the sacraments that constitute the Church.

In the Church of England these groups of people are not 'congregational' because they are in fellowship with other congregations in the diocese and the province through the bishop and archbishop. Nor do they have an independent church order; they are bound by the constitution of the Church of England; this constitution is established by law, as we have seen, and the clergy of each congregation are under the same Canons of that constitution. Each congregation also shares a liturgy which is common to all other similar congregations. Thus each congregation is part of the national Church.

But late in the life of the Church of England synodical government has evolved; parishes elect to deanery synods, deaneries elect to diocesan synods, dioceses elect to the General Synod. It has good points and it has bad points. It is good in that it provides a machinery for communication between bishops, clergy and laity at national, regional, and sub-regional levels. It is bad because often those involved in these structures think that 'the Church' can be identified with the synods — whether it be the General Synod, the Diocesan Synod or the Deanery Synod. But these synods are just structures where representatives of the various *churches* can meet and discuss. They have no on-going life apart from the parish churches. Indeed, if there were no parish churches — if they became extinct — there would be no deaneries, no dioceses and no Church of England!

It can therefore be said that if the Church of England is to become more effective, we will have to see some massive growth in the parish churches of our land. And the parish churches should be strengthened and grow in four ways: first, in numerical strength as more people are converted or become truly committed to Jesus Christ; second, in spiritual depth and genuineness of worship; third, in their quality of fellowship; and, fourth, in their impact on the society around.

Training lay leaders

There will, however, be no growth unless the leadership base in each place is increased. This is the 'Pyramid Principle' we have already referred to. But training *lay* leaders for growth in the Church is no easier than training clergy.

Yes, in a new church recently planted, it is not too difficult. There is a 'clean slate'. But in well-established churches it is harder.

First, it is hard to persuade some people who already have been involved in the church for a number of years that they may well have to be retrained! But if the church is to grow, these people will need to relate their previous experience to where the Church is now going. And some 'old hands' have got so used to doing a job in *their* way that they find it hard to readjust.

For example, in a church of seventy at morning worship the volunteers serving tea after the service can be very relaxed. They can chat with people as they serve tea and pastoral work can even be done 'at the hatch'. But if the church is to grow or is growing to a hundred and fifty, that is not possible. The 'loving' action is to serve the tea as fast as possible so that others are not waiting unduly. Pastoral conversations have to take place at another time. A trivial example, but this principle holds in so many areas. If a church grows, welcoming, hospitality, pastoral care, teaching and education all have to be much more *intentional* and thought through. This is what we mean by management. But management involves ensuring that people are trained for the situation *as it is becoming.*

Secondly, it is hard to generate a consciousness of growth in a small church before it has started to grow. 'Why bother with training?' is the response of some. This is particularly so when people treat 'church' as a weekend activity — like going to the theatre. But if you put high demands upon people, it will often make them realize that what you are doing is serious. The parable of the mustard seed is always to be remembered. Growth begins small.

At our own church, when I first came to Jesmond in 1973, I decided that it was essential to develop the creche for babies during the morning service. There were only a few babies then, but a new room was obviously required. And it had to be carpeted and warm. Soon more helpers were needed, for with better facilities and a more systematic approach, new families started coming with new babies. My wife then took charge and began some training. Over the years through written material and training evenings (with the use of films etc), she has made it clear what the expectations are and how the creche relates to the rest of the church. But the way of operating has had to change as the creche has grown — from three or four babies to thirty and from five on the rota to fifty. And further changes, we trust, will be necessary in the interests of growth and improvement. Similar changes and the need for new ways of working could be illustrated from many other areas of our work.

Douglas W. Johnson says there are three pressures of and for change that require attention in the development of training programmes: first, changes keep happening in the growing church as the goals change; second, people change jobs in the church; and third, skills need to be changed and upgraded.[1] But it all takes time.

Staffing for growth

Once a Church takes the ministry of every member seriously, there will be a need for *more* not less full-time staff in a Church. This conclusion means that the proposals and recommendations of the ACCM Report *A Strategy for the Church's Ministry* by John Tiller have to be radically questioned.[2] His scenario for the future is of cells or groups of lay people serviced by diocesan 'teams' of full-timers. However, studies from other parts of the world would indicate that a withdrawal, or reduction in the number, of full-time workers from local congregations is a recipe for decline not growth. It was conspicuous that in the Report there was no mention of the arguments against this sort of strategy that are in the literature on Church organization and development published, particularly in the United States, over the past decade.

Volunteer (as distinct from stipendary) lay ministry is not a solution to the problem of too few full-timers. But because volunteers enable the Church to be effective (when they are trained and co-ordinated) they are a solution to the problem of the ineffectiveness of the Church. It needs to be repeated that once volunteer lay ministry is successful in a church, there will be a need for *more* full-time staff to co-ordinate, train and provide back-up services.

This has been my experience at Jesmond. I started with two

and a half staff; we now have eight and four halves. Our latest appointment was that of a youth co-ordinator. We currently have 140–150 under eighteens in our Sunday youth programmes. There are midweek activities as well. But the time and energy required in recruiting, training and coordinating the many volunteer leaders involved in these youth programmes meant we needed extra 'man hours' being put in *by one person* from somewhere. As there is a finite amount of time volunteers can give, sometimes you have to buy those man/woman hours.

An interesting parallel to the Church situation was drawn to my attention some years ago by a member of the congregation who teaches law in the University of Newcastle-upon-Tyne. He reported that in one of the Scandinavian countries there has been a 'lay' form of probation. Those put on probation are assigned to certain 'lay' people in the community instead of professional probation officers. And there has been evidence of its success. So why cannot it be used in this country? Because it seemed that to operate such a system demanded *more* full-time probation personnel; and so initially it costs more money! These full-time probation workers are required for training and back-up services. The system is effective. But it is not a quick solution to a shortage of probation officers.

This is precisely the situation in the Church. That is why the current shortfall in ordinands is so very serious. It is no good the Church planning to organize itself for the end of the twentieth century on the basis of a shortage of full-time workers. Rather it needs to apply itself to the biblical mandate of praying for more (many more) full-time church workers. Jesus once said to his disciples: 'The harvest is plentiful, but the labourers are few; pray therefore the Lord of the harvest to send out labourers into his harvest' (Mt 9:37-38). To plan to do nothing and to accept the status quo is to plan for decline. And we will surely get it! It was Robert Schuller who said, 'I would rather attempt something great for God and fail than attempt nothing for God and succeed'.

Team ministry

If a congregation is going to see growth, a team of staff will
have to develop. However, they will not, by virtue of being
full-time, automatically form the senior leadership of the
Church. Perhaps the first extra full-timer will be a secretary,
rather than another senior pastoral person. The full-time staff
are to be seen as resource people. They could be specialists in
pastoral care, youth work or administration. Some will be
senior leaders, but even they will probably be working with
other volunteer senior leaders. It is important to note that this
is a team serving *one* congregation. It is based on *one* worship
centre. And it works under *one* senior clergyman — a vicar.
Such a team can help the church to grow.

This is a model that is developing around the country. One
indication is the growth of *Administry*.[3] *Administry* was an
organization set up by John Truscott, a former church administrator at St Helen's, Bishopsgate, to promote church administration. Not unnaturally a large proportion of the churches
involved in the project are those with full-time administrators.
But now *Administry* has grown to such a size that its own staff
is being increased; and this is because parish administrators
throughout the country have grown in number. Two conferences of *Administry* at present have to be run in parallel — one in
the North and one in the South.

But something must be noted: the team that has been outlined above is not what is usually meant by Team Ministry in
the Church of England. Ever since the *Pastoral Measure* of
1968 you can have a team from joining together a number of
parishes into a single benefice, but the parishes don't disband.
You then have a team rector appointed as the leader of a team
of team vicars.

Theoretically, there seems to be some value in the clergy of
small churches forming such an association. But the value has
yet to be proved. Indeed, such studies as have been done
would suggest that teaming in this way may often inhibit
church growth. The Report by the Ministry Co-ordinating

Group *Team and Group Ministries* published by the General Synod in 1985 nowhere asks the question, 'Do teams lead to numerical growth?'

This is a necessary question, because the conclusion of Lyle Schaller is that 'intercongregational cooperation in programming is incompatible with numerical growth.'[4] He is an American Methodist, a consultant with the Yokefellow Institute and a leading authority on church planning. He has analysed thousands of churches and describes facing and accepting this conclusion as a 'repugnant tradeoff in developing a church strategy'. It is 'repugnant' because it runs counter to received ministerial wisdom.

And you can see three reasons why he is probably right.

First, lines of responsibility can get tangled when several *separate* congregations are trying to cooperate under an intercongregational leadership.

Second, once you start cooperating with other people outside your immediate communications network, precious time and energy are consumed. This is time and energy *not* spent in fostering contacts with those totally outside the Christian faith. It is time and energy not spent in training and in other activities that will lead to the greater effectiveness of members. Obviously small congregations, before they have grown, will have to cooperate for some purposes; and all congregations sometimes will want to do so for *limited* ventures; but these are not to be viewed as *permanent* arrangements, as they use up extra time and energy.

Third, cooperation easily becomes an end in itself.

It may well be that in certain rural areas Anglican teams are necessary. But the Church of England should provide hard evidence that teams lead to church growth before a lot more teaming of separate parishes is encouraged. If teaming is just to provide for *clergy* needs, that must be admitted. But there are other ways of meeting *those* needs.

What seems preferable is for urban churches to grow and develop teams *within the 'one' structure*.

Synods

In the case of what Anglicans officially mean by team ministries, we have to beware of the danger of spending time and energy on 'lateral communication', for the Church is not called primarily to communicate with other churches. It is called to communicate with the world about God, and with God about the world.

However, an increasing amount of time is spent by Anglicans on inter-church dialogue. I refer to synodical government.

It is of course vitally necessary that Christians relate to one another, encourage one another and care for one another, but this is to be as the 'body of Christ' — as they worship together, pray together, share around the Lord's table together and meet together. It is thus a function of *the parish congregation*. This cannot be done as a deanery or a diocese or as the national church. Out of a congregation of hundreds there may only be four lay people on the Deanery Synod. So if the deanery was responsible for ministry, the majority of lay people would never get ministered to! And only some of the deanery members are on the Diocesan Synod; and only a few of the Diocesan Synod members are on the General Synod. These synods are simply a means of communication, a means of generating structures and a means of channelling advice. The *work* of the Church of England is and can only be done, fundamentally, at the parish level.

Currently there is some disquiet about synodical government in the Church. Why? There are five reasons at least.

First, there are sometimes wrong expectations. Some people both on and off the synods have a much greater sense of their importance than is warranted. Synods can't *get things done*. In a 'voluntary, non-profit' organization, a decision of a committee, council or synod cannot effect change unless it is genuinely reflecting changes (or the desire for change) 'down below'. This is even true of a parochial church council.

A PCC can vote that the church should have a larger youth work. But that decision is irrelevant until a decision is actually taken by a person to give up precious time for the regular

Sunday Bible teaching class, a regular Saturday night social event, summer CYFA and Pathfinder camps and houseparties, national CYFA training conferences, regional training conferences, weekly, fortnightly or monthly local leaders meetings.

But the further removed from the parish you get, often the more unrealistic are the expectations of what can be achieved. It may be reported that 'the Diocese has decided this' or 'the General Synod has decided that'. But in terms of Church advance these decisions can never *actually* get growth to occur. At best, they are structural decisions to enable work to happen in the parishes, *other things being equal*. And of course, if they are the *wrong* decisions, they can also disable parish life.

Time, information and 'shape'

The second problem is the time the synods consume. Of course, there must be synodical committees and boards. But too many absorb precious time and energy. The net result is often that good people in the parishes are unwilling to spend time on them. If they are involved in a growing church they will already be engaged in extra local church activities for training. They will be involved in visiting, pastoral care, youth work, nurture groups, home groups etc. This means that those with good judgement as to what *works* in a parish and contributes to its growth are often not present on the synods.

Perhaps such lay activities haven't yet started in a church. But they never will if all the good people and potential workers have much of their spare time already taken up in deanery and diocesan affairs.

The third problem with synodical government is that so often there is insufficient information to make judgements. For example, when a Synod discusses, say, team ministry, probably no evidence will be provided on the relationship between team ministry and growth. Yet the Synod is asked there and then to endorse the Pastoral Committee's plan for more teams in the Diocese! No one can be blamed. The Diocesan office is not staffed like a Civil Service department. But some people operate as though it was.

The fourth problem relates to the 'shape' of the Church. What do we mean by 'shape'? — the detailed profile of a church that takes account of its size, the tenure of its membership, the sex and age ratios, the social class, its geography and its churchmanship. We can easily distinguish churches by *size* — those, for example, with 50, 150, 450, 600 or more at worship. They are radically different organizations. Their needs are different. Their strengths and weaknesses are different.

But then we can also distinguish churches by the *tenure of their membership* — how long members of the congregation have been worshippers at that church. We can also distinguish *age and sex* — one church is mostly females over 60, another is married couples over 45, another is young married couples. Then there is *social class* — that is also important. Then there is *geographical location* — rural, suburban middle class, suburban working class, new housing estate, inner city, central city. And finally there is *churchmanship*.

But policies and programmes appropriate to a church of one shape are irrelevant, if not positively harmful, to a church of another shape. But so much deanery, diocesan and General Synod planning assumes that the only difference between churches is *churchmanship*. Otherwise all are the same. That is foolish; but it is the danger of any organization that gets too centralized, for centralization often means that standard solutions have to be offered to very different problems.

A case in point is the parsonage. The Church Commissioners may decide that a vicarage ought to be of so many square feet. That may suit some suburban parishes, but in some rural areas, the vicarage has to double as a creche and Sunday School facility. To reduce its size means that the creche or the youth group have nowhere to meet. In central-city parishes some vicarages also house office facilities that are essential to the work of the church.

Doctrinal disagreement

The fifth problem of synodical government is doctrinal disagreement. This is quite fundamental. Because there is such deep theological division in the Church of England, synodical discussions, whether at the deanery, diocesan or General Synod level, often end up 're-inventing the wheel', theologically speaking. But if there cannot be agreement on what is to be believed, total frustration is inevitable. Indeed, many members of synods, committees, boards and councils are very frustrated because there is no common agreement over goals or methods of procedure. For example, some people may have what others reckon a cavalier attitude towards the Bible and the traditional wisdom of the Church; these others say that the Bible, confirmed by Christian tradition, must be our guideline. How can they all ever really agree?

This seemed to be happening in 1979 with the Bishop of Gloucester's Working Party on homosexual relationships. The Working Party wanted to say, 'There are circumstances in which individuals may justifiably choose to enter into a homosexual relationship.'[5] Many members of the Board for Social Responsibility disagreed. The reason was a fundamental disagreement theologically.

The Bishop of Gloucester wrote in his Preface to the Working Party's Report:

> We have not brushed aside what the Bible has to say about sexuality, we have indeed taken great pains to interpret it rightly. On the other hand, we have not felt bound simply to repeat its every utterance.[6]

But the Board for Social Responsibility under the Bishop of London felt that this rejection of the Church's traditional teaching was due to a less than serious attitude to the Bible:

> An interpretation is often put upon the biblical text which gives the impression that the conclusion came first and influenced the way in which the evidence was interpreted.[7]

In the end one and the same volume, *Homosexual Relationships — a contribution to discussion* contained a Working Party Report saying one thing and the Board for Social Responsibility saying almost the very opposite. This is both confusing and frustrating.

15

Geared for growth

Most Anglican churches are small. According to the Nation-wide Initiative in Evangelism survey 28 per cent had under 25 in the congregation; 61 per cent had between 26–150; 10 per cent had 151–300; and 1 per cent 301–500; (over 500 were too few to be statistically significant). Nine out of every ten Anglican churches have under 150. If the individual worshipping congregation is our frame of reference, the small church is clearly the most numerous.

But if the focus is changed from counting congregations to looking at the actual experience of worship of members of the Church of England, we have a different picture. The survey showed that on average 50 per cent of worshipping Anglicans in the country will be found in 20 per cent of the churches; and a third of all worshipping Anglicans will be found in just one-tenth of the churches.

What is the significance of this? First, this is not peculiar to the Church of England. In the Episcopal Church in the United States one-third of all Episcopal parishes account for approximately three-quarters of all practising Episcopalians.

Secondly, these statistics tell us where Anglicans are to be found. Half of them are to be found in a small proportion of the churches. If we are concerned with *actual people*, half our time, energy and money ought to be spent in a concern with a proportionately smaller number of larger churches.

Thirdly, they may have something to say about deployment of manpower. In the mainline denominations in the United States, where the overall statistics are not very different from those in the United Kingdom, it has been discovered that it is 15 per cent of the churches (not 20 per cent as in the Church of England) that reach 50 per cent of the membership; while 50 per cent of the churches serve only 15 per cent of the membership. *Yet the distribution of clergy serving these two groups is about equally divided;* about as many pastors work with the 15 per cent (the large churches with half the denominational membership), as work with 50 per cent of congretions (the small churches with less than one-fifth of the denominational membership). The bishops need to check that it is not the same in the Church of England. Such information is necessary for assessing the *Sheffield Quota* (the number of clergy for each diocese) and deployment generally.

But, that being said, as the small church is characteristic of the Church of England, and growth is our goal, we must consider how the small Anglican church can begin to grow.

Helping the small church to grow

How can a small church in the Church of England grow? Five preliminary comments need to be made.

First, we need to answer those who think that this sort of statistical analysis is improper in discussing the Church. They acknowledge that the Church is a theological reality; they acknowledge that it is a historical reality; but they are not so sure about the suggestion that it is a sociological reality. Perhaps they can be reassured by the conviction that *grace perfects and does not destroy nature.* The Church consists of redeemed men and women, but the men and women are still *human* both in their individual and communal lives. So principles of normal human interaction will usually be as true of the Church's life as they are of society in general. The distinguishing marks of the Church's communal life should be interaction by love and the fruit of the Spirit!

Second, to take Schumacher's phrase, 'small is beautiful'. After all, the small church is one of the oldest forms of the local church. The early Church met in homes — true, sometimes large homes; but many must have been small churches.

Third, small churches can grow. It is often assumed that all small churches must remain small. This was not the experience of the small churches in the early centuries. Of course, some churches in areas of low or *de*-population may have permanently limiting factors. However, they can still become missionary or 'church planting' as we shall see. But for many small churches, given adequate faith, self-understanding and strategy, there is no reason why they shouldn't grow. Around the world such churches are growing. Why not in the United Kingdom?

The trouble with many small churches is that they have a low level of corporate self-esteem. As Lyle Schaller puts it:

> Frequently the members of these congregations see themselves as small, weak, unattractive, powerless, and frustrated with a limited future. That self-image often creates a self-perpetuating cycle that produces policies and decisions that inhibit the potential outreach. Their priorities are survival and institutional maintenance, not evangelism.[1]

Fourth, the reason why some small churches do not grow may be spiritual, *but not necessarily*. They may need to revise their theology and come more alive to God. They may need to be more committed. But Schaller makes this cautionary comment:

> After interviewing lay persons from over five thousand congregations including hundreds of leaders from small churches, I have found no evidence to suggest that the commitment to Jesus Christ as Lord and Saviour is any less among the members of the small-membership churches than it is among the members of rapidly growing churches.[2]

Fifth, we must not view a small church as just a church with a small number of people in it. A small church is distinguished from a middle-sized church not so much by its numerical size, but by its *social structure*. A small church is fundamentally a 'single cell' church. Let George Hunter explain:

> A church that is essentially a *single cell*, in which virtually all the members regularly interact with almost all the others, is rightly designated a 'small' church. *Multicell* churches, where a given member interacts with some members all the time, but with others only occasionally or rarely, are not by this definition small churches.[3]

It is true that a number of 'small' churches 'stretch' their 'single cells' to a size larger than you would expect; but they are still large single cells.

Growing with difficulty

The holding power of the small church is very great indeed. It meets some basic human needs including that for order in life. This is because a small church is so often always the same. That is attractive and reassuring.

As the typical small church is an overgrown small group, it has certain priorities. It is these that make growth difficult. The members want a small-group experience of face-to-face contact. They are not so much interested in goals, or a well-managed structure, or programmes appropriate to modern urban needs. They put a high price on the quality of inter-personal relationships. They will, therefore, resist anything that looks like eroding the strength of these relationships.

That is the reason why you cannot, in terms of church planning, put a number of existing small churches together and make them into a larger one. It cannot be done just like that. And that is the reason why growth is hard. For the small church to grow, there has to be a trade-off. Carl Dudley sums it up: 'A small church cannot grow in membership size without giving up its most precious appeal, its intimacy.'[4] Its 'intimacy' is the basic satisfaction that everyone knows, or knows about, everyone else.

But let us assume that a small church has begun to face up to this issue and that they are willing to consider evangelism. What then? How can it start to grow?

It is vital that the church is dependent on the Holy Spirit to guide and equip. Of course, prayer must be the context of every strategy. But there are four other strategies that can be employed in the case of small churches that want to begin to grow: one, focusing on Christ's commission; two, multiplying cells; three, having a new (or renewed) vicar; and, four, 'building bridges'.

Strategy number one is to encourage the membership to focus on the words of Christ's 'Great Commission' recorded in Matthew 28:19, that we should 'go . . . and make disciples of all nations.' This is all inclusive and covers all those *outside* the Church. Few in a small church would really be motivated for growth who did not believe in the 'lostness of the lost'! This is theological and another indication of how a church that is confused theologically is unlikely to grow. But assuming theological consensus, what then?

Strategy number two is to attempt to multiply cells. But that will require a preliminary educational exercise.

For, first, the members of a small 'single cell' congregation need to realize that a multiple-cell church can be healthy, whereas remaining a single-cell church is unhealthy. This is simply because remaining as a single-cell church imposes limits on outreach! Being so tightly knit, it is much harder for outsiders to break into the life of a single-cell church.

Second, as we have already suggested, the membership needs to realize that a small church cannot always minister adequately in a complex society and usually will be very weak in regard to youth work.

But, third, and most important of all, the members of a small church need to realize that the values they so cherish in the small church *can* be experienced in the larger congregation. True, it won't happen automatically. There has to be conscious planning on the part of the leadership to ensure the mainten-ance of small units within the growing church, which will still hold people. But experience proves that in a multicell con-gregation, each person can still be related to as many people as in a single-cell congregation. Meaningful fellowship can be maintained; and generally the long-standing members will continue to relate to each other.

New groups

Perhaps the easiest way of developing a multicell congregation is the creation of new groups in the church. One or two members may start a Bible discussion group for outreach; or, as we have at Jesmond and a number of other churches now have, beginners groups (we call them Mustard Seed Groups). These are for people who either are uncommitted and are wanting to ask questions, or for people who have just become Christians and who want to sort out further some issues of belief, or for people who are already committed but want to go back to basics.

In a small church, the group can be allowed to continue after a set course has finished. Often the fellowship built up is so strong that there is a resistance to disbanding. In a larger church sometimes it is necessary to encourage people to enter other fellowship groups at this point. But even in larger churches it is sometimes useful to have a follow-on course. We have developed 'Mustard Shoot' courses. At the end of such a period you have a new cell!

A small church can develop other forms of cell life. Where there is a will in a church, there is usually a way. But it takes time, effort and training. If your key leaders who could start cells are always off to deanery or diocesan meetings, you have a problem! In a small church it is usually just those people who have to go to such meetings — there is no one else to go. It is then a matter of priorities. But if the small church opts out of 'cell multiplication' it is unlikely to have the satisfaction of obeying Christ's 'Great Commission'; they will not have the satisfaction of sharing something they have been privileged to receive with people who, in fact, are desperate to receive it!

A new vicar

One of the difficulties a small church faces over growing is that the initiative to help often won't come from inside. In an urban area a number of the members of a small church quite possibly will say, 'If I wanted our church to be a big one, I would be going somewhere else.'

Nor must we delude ourselves that in urban areas parochial boundaries are vitally significant. The primary community for many *men* is not based on where they sleep but on where they work, on their social life and leisure activities and on family connections. In urban areas it is mainly young mothers who have the greatest attachment to the locality. They develop relationships with other local young mothers at the school gate. That is one of the reasons why in the parochial setting work among young mothers is usually easier than work among their husbands and among young men generally.

Thus, because parochial boundaries often are not absolute, for many people attachment to (or detachment from!) the small church has been a matter of choice. For some it is a choice that they prefer something larger and so have voted with their feet; and that is why the church is very small. For others there has been a positive choice for a small church. For yet others the choice has been simply to stay put. These are the less confident members of the small church, who would like something different, but the trauma of uprooting themselves and moving is too great. They certainly are not strong enough to initiate change.

But the Church does not exist for the benefit only of its members. It must be growth-orientated. The only hope, therefore, in such situations is when the vicar has a turn-around and a radically new awareness of the possibilities of growth. He becomes aware that Christ calls us not just to 'feed sheep' but to 'catch fish'. He sees that being a vicar and exercising leadership for growth is a very sophisticated and exciting task. He becomes enthusiastic about his small church growing. He realizes that while principles may apply across the board, no two churches are alike. He has no intention of imitating the big church in the middle of town. But he sees the potential for change in his small church. Quite realistically he is not expecting it all to be different in the morning! But he begins to recognize the truth of the proposition that 'most clergy overestimate what they can achieve in one year and underestimate what they can achieve in five years'.

With such a 'renewed' vicar the small church has leadership for a change. Otherwise it may have to wait for a change of incumbent. That is why *strategy number three* for small church growth is for there to be a new (or renewed) vicar.

Nor, if the church has to wait for a new incumbent, does that mean that the church may be critical of the existing vicar. The current incumbent may well be doing a preparatory job. Many churches that experience the greatest growth are building on the foundations laid by someone else who had unacknowledged gifts. But Schaller makes the general point:

> Most of the long-tenure members [in a small church] lack the skills, the time, the desire, the authority, or the energy to initiate a strategy for change. Therefore, the likeliest candidate to initiate this strategy is the just-arrived 'new minister', who possesses the freedom of the outsider, still has some discretionary time in every month, holds authority that goes with the office of pastor, has no stake in maintaining the status quo, possesses a strong evangelistic concern, and has gifts and skills in the process of planned change.[5]

Evangelism in the small church

Strategy number four for small church growth is to function properly and to enable bridges to be built. Let me explain.

Small church people are not by nature evangelistic. They are warmhearted and good at hospitality; but aggressive evangelism is not their gift. It is not that they do not want to see men and women won to Jesus Christ, but they tremble at the thought of becoming evangelistic. Hunter writes:

> They balk because they equate evangelism with visiting strangers on their turf, verbalizing the gospel and eliciting a response in one transaction, and then assimilating these responding strangers into their single-cell church.[6]

But one of the lessons that those studying church growth have discovered in recent years is that outreach to strangers is not necessary for people to be converted and assimilated into the Church.

Indeed, what is being recovered is a more biblical pattern of evangelism. Evangelism is seen as a function not just of the individual but of the whole Church. As St Paul says:

> Speaking the truth in love, we are to grow up in every way into him who is the head, into Christ, from whom the whole body, joined and knit together by every joint with which it is supplied, *when each part is working properly,* makes bodily growth and upbuilds itself in love (Eph 4:15-16).

That has been my experience over the years. The quality of the care in the creche, the condition of the toilets, the friendliness of sidesmen, the attractiveness of the flowers, the liveliness of the music, the effort put in by the vicar and other staff in preparing business meetings *as well as* the essential duties of the church in front-line evangelism, preaching, teaching, pastoral care and appropriate social and political involvement, are all integral to the growth of the church. And there needs to be a 'climate of love', prayer and expectancy for the Holy Spirit to work.

The goal, of course, is not to 'get decisions', but 'to make disciples'. That is to say, men and women have to be built up and helped to function in the local church, the body of Christ. Evangelism is, therefore, a 'total' process. But there should be many points of entry into the Christian fellowship and for commitment to Jesus Christ.

Growth obviously needs those with the gift of evangelism being freed to function. And perhaps more have that gift than realize it: the first qualification, many would say, is not the ability to speak but the ability to listen. You can then apply the gospel to real needs.

Growth also needs new converts being encouraged to evangelize. They are usually quite effective. It is the experience of many churches that in the early phase of a new convert's life, communication bridges with those 'outside' are still strong. In time, however, these old links weaken. But in a church where there is a continuous programme of evangelism, new converts are always replacing the old.

But does all this mean that the established members of the congregation, who do not feel called to evangelize, are consigned only to making the tea and polishing the brass (necessary as these tasks are)? No!

This is because fewer people are outside the orbit of the Church than we imagine. For we are all in relationship with a number of people. Our church decline is often due to our failure to use the 'bridges' that are quite open to each one of us. Indeed, it would be most unusual if there were not responsive people in our own existing networks of social relationships: they will be relatives, friends, neighbours and colleagues at work.

Using 'bridges' and social networks

Research has shown that most new church members come through personal invitation. A Gallup Poll of churchgoers showed that 58 per cent of those who now go to church regularly, first began going when they were invited by *someone they knew*. Conversely, 63 per cent of those who do not go to church say that none of their friends or acquaintances has ever invited them.

Winfield Arn conducted a survey of 4,000 converts. He wanted to find out how they got into contact with the Church. His findings were these: *between three-quarters of these new Christians were invited to church by relatives and friends;* about one in ten were attracted by the clergyman; fewer just walked in; about 3 per cent each, came through the churches' programmes; or because of a special need; or through a Bible-study group by itself. Less than two per cent came through being visited by church members.[7]

Of course, programmes, meeting needs and all the rest of the Church's life is vital once a person is in relationship with a church. But the initial invitation is so fundamental.

Donald McGavran tells of a Mennonite church in Japan. This has been for many years the fastest-growing congregation of its denomination in that country. It has one principle of church growth — postconversion training.

One evening every week for three months a new convert receives this training, on a one-to-one basis in the new convert's home. The convert's family is invited to join in if they wish (this is all part of the 'social network' strategy). For a few minutes each evening the trainer and convert list names of relatives, friends, neighbours and colleagues at work. At the end of three months every contact of the new convert should have been identified. Those not in any church are then marked and the trainer asks: 'Which of these do you have influence with?' These are then made into a final list and are visited by *both* the convert *and* the trainer. The convert simply says what has been happening in his life and the trainer tries to explain something of the gospel. He then leaves a Bible portion or a booklet. The person is invited to church or some special event. If interest is shown there is a further visit. The goal is for that person to come to a living faith in Jesus Christ.[8]

There are other ways of using our social networks. In the Full Gospel Central Church in Seoul some people make a habit in their tower blocks of simply trying to identify practical needs through continual use of the lifts! They then help in the name of Christ and share the gospel as appropriate. This is a natural practical bridge. But it takes time and energy, as well as imagination. Growth is always costly.

16

Church planting and finance

In his *The Anglican Church Today and Tomorrow* Bishop
Michael Marshall spoke of 'a strong need to break loose and
to encourage an alternative Church — a more gathered Church
alongside the parochial and community Churches of the past'.[1]
He also mentions 'alternative patterns of the gathered Church,
at all sorts of times and in all sorts of places'.[2] His conclusion
is that 'alongside many continuing traditional practices of
Anglicanism, there simply must be some radical ingredients
of change if Anglicanism, humanly speaking, is to survive
into the next century'.[3]

We have already seen that the Church of England (along
with the other denominations) is experiencing numerical
decline. The proposal of many Christian strategists is that
there has to be what Donald McGavran has called 'a renaissance of new Church extension'. Thousands of new churches
need to be planted.

Church planting

'But don't we already have 53,000 churches in this country if
we total all the denominations throughout the United Kingdom (not just England)? Aren't they enough for these islands?
Don't we need *better* churches and *stronger* cooperation,
rather than *more* churches?'

When we look at the evidence I believe the answer is clearly 'No'! We do need *more* churches; so we need to plant them.

If we follow Donald McGavran's reasoning there are three lines of evidence we need to follow up. So let me transpose the sort of arguments he uses in his essay *Reaching people through new congregations*[4] and put them in terms of the United Kingdom.

First, new congregations are more 'evangelistically prolific' than old ones. Lyle Schaller reports:

> New church development . . . is the most effective means for reaching unchurched persons. Numerous studies have shown that 60 to 80 per cent of the new adult members of new congregations are persons who were not actively involved in the life of any worshipping congregation immediately prior to joining that new mission. By contrast, most long established Churches draw the majority of their new adult members from persons who transfer in from other congregations.[5]

Second, sheer numbers prove we need thousands of new churches for new Christians. The vast *unchurched* population of the United Kingdom demands millions more Christians. For these we shall need all the existing churches and thousands of new churches. Huge numbers of British people are without any real church connection or link. The population of the United Kingdom is 56 million. Of this number 11 million are practising Christians (and 'on the books' even though they won't all be present every Sunday!). There are, therefore, 45 million outside the Church. Of these 45 million, 32 million might consider themselves 'religious' or 'nominally Christian'. The remaining 13 million are positively 'non-Christian' — Marxists, humanists etc.

One of the problems is that many church leaders have a false impression that their communities are much more heavily churched than they really are. In a few areas where there is a population decrease that may be true. But in one study it has been found that if the population is not decreasing, the larger the number of congregations per thousand residents, the higher the proportion of churchgoers. And the figures prove that nationally we are not over churched.

The United Kingdom has a population of 56 million. There are 53,000 churches in all. As we have seen, most congregations are small. According to the NIE survey, on Tyneside the average size of a Protestant congregation is 63. But just supposing each church had a sudden revival of religion and had now on average 200 regular church attenders as members. *That would only give 10·6 million practising Christians in the country* (a figure lower than our original number of allegedly 'practising' Christians: that indicates the measure of the problem and the commitment of 'members on the books'). *And there would still be 45·4 million on that reckoning who were outside the Church.* Whatever the precise details this fact remains: enormous numbers of our fellow countrymen have yet to become committed to Christ and to responsible membership of his Church.

Cultural distance

We are not referring to buildings in the first instance when we refer to a new church. For these fellow countrymen may well be put off by some of the buildings. But if we are to reach them it will only be by new approaches and new churches. This relates to our third line of evidence in favour of church planting — the problem of culture.

It is culturally necessary that we plant new churches. McGavran writes:

> As generation succeeds generation most denominations settle into cultural forms of worship usually quite appropriate to the people they have become.[6]

This produces a dignified procedure for the worship of God. It is quiet and reverent and has music in a classical style usually on an organ. Generally speaking it is an aesthetic worship experience. It is predominantly middle class and for a small section of the middle class at that. But since only a small part of the total community fits worship forms like this, it is too easy to assume either that we should only evangelize people who like our kind of experience, or that when people reject 'our church', they are necessarily rejecting the gospel.

Worship must be expressed in the heart language of the subculture we are aiming to reach in our evangelism — that is, if members of that subculture are really to involve themselves in the worship and become disciples and not merely those who make decisions for Christ.

So that is why a crucial question for any church committed to growth is this: 'Are we willing to import less elevated ways of worshipping if this is the way to win large numbers of the British "working" class (or any other group for that matter)?' Most would say 'No!' Nor is this always culpable, for it would in many cases require such a degree of forced change that the result would be wholly false and inappropriate.

It is a simple fact that the 'redemption and lift' (the phenomenon recognized by John Wesley that we have already referred to) tends to cut churches off from huge sections of the society around them. Millions, therefore, live too far away culturally, liturgically or geographically from even the liveliest of our churches. And even if we won all we could into existing churches, millions would be left outside. *For them we need new churches*.

How do we start?

How do we begin to implement a policy of church planting? What about parish boundaries? What about finance? What about leadership?

First, we must establish that the priority must always be the needs of the unchurched rather than the needs of the Church of England for more members. Secondly, we can be encouraged by the fact that having identified these needs, a newly planted church is able to develop a response to needs, rather than a response to the pressures of yesterday's traditions. Thirdly, we must have confidence from the fact that most people like being in at the creation of something new.

But practically how do you begin? There is now much

experience from all over the world on church planting, and a considerable literature. Some of the accumulated wisdom relates to the 'church planter' himself. This is a distinct gift. Many would advise that one person on their own, or with at most one other, takes the initiative, for if you have sections of congregations hiving off, with a reasonable number being sent out from a mother church, they tend to reduplicate their existing cultural patterns in the new congregation.

The Americans have wide experience of church planting. The Pentecostal Assemblies of God have been starting well over 200 congregations per year. The Southern Baptists have been starting 700 a year! A typical way they work is to find a highly motivated, entrepreneurial, person-centred, extroverted clergyman. Besides being a man of prayer and faith, he will be someone who has a desire to succeed, willing for sacrifices, prepared to take risks, independent, optimistic, and prepared to solve problems rather than look for 'a scapegoat'. Rather cynically Schaller says such people 'are unlike most of the students enrolling in denominational seminaries.'[7]

Having found the man, he is sent out to spend half a year to a year meeting as many people as possible and developing friendship ties. Energy is concentrated on those without any active church connection. At least six calls would be made on each person before any suggested 'worship event' took place. And that would only be laid on when it was clear a good number would respond to the invitation.

The North East Diocesan Evangelical Fellowship said in its *Position* (see Appendix 1): 'We are strongly convinced . . . that new churches need to be planted in areas where the historic Christian faith has not penetrated'. It was suggested that there should be 'as a goal, after research, a significant number of new "worship centres" of at least 100 members each in the North East by 1990.' It is certain that there are parishes where church planting would be welcomed. A model suggested on Tyneside was to set apart a person for one year for 'research'. For the two succeeding years, he would make contact 'from outside' the target area. In the next two years he and his wife would live in the area, but still be supported from outside. After five years there should be an 'indigenous' church of 100 and little external support.

There are many other models of working, however. Technicalities are at this stage not important. The primary need is to establish goals, and get agreement on goals. 'New churches' can be formed by 'out-post' home groups or bible-study groups — early Methodism started like that. In Latin America people use restaurants, hotels and other public places as preaching points. Why should Anglicans assume that this strategy in England is only open to the house churches? If necessary you can open up a second congregation in the same building. This is what happened in Victorian Britain. The well-to-do went in the morning, their servants went in the evening, when there might be a more informal way of worshipping. Most of us find this distasteful and 'sub-Christian'; but we have to be careful that we don't let a proper worry about social divisions prejudice us from modern experiments that are designed to help the underprivileged. And, of course, old-fashioned 'daughter churches' are a perfectly good way of church planting.

Money — the fourth quarter

But how are new churches to pay their way? Money, sooner or later, comes onto the agenda of every Christian strategy. The Bible has much to say about money and about giving. Three quarters of our problems about money come from our not taking the Bible seriously in its teaching on money. After all it was Jesus who said, 'It is more blessed to give than to receive' (Acts 20:35). Our giving is first to be a giving of ourselves to God, then of our money in a response to his great gift in Jesus Christ. And as we give, so quite remarkably, God blesses us (even sometimes materially): 'He who sows sparingly will also reap sparingly, and he who sows bountifully will also reap bountifully' (2 Cor 9:6).

There undoubtedly is enough money in the Church of

England to see a huge expansion of the Christian movement in our country. The problem is that it is locked away in the purses, wallets, bank accounts, investments, savings and property of its members. The wealth of the Church is not in the Church Commissioners' assets, nor in the various funds of the Diocesan Boards of Finance, nor in the PCC accounts. These are simply 'liquid assets' providing a cash flow for the purposes of mission and ministry. The problem is getting all these resources out of pockets and banks and then turning this money into mission and ministry.

How well is the Church of England doing that? Judging by the disproportionate amount of time deaneries talk about the 'quota' (the amount each local church raises for central finance), not very well. The 'facts' are hard to come by. Being a 'voluntary, non-profit' organization and, therefore, not with the powers of the Inland Revenue, there is no real way you can tell if people are giving or not. You can do some calculations, such as dividing the income of a parish by the church's electoral roll. You then get a per capita figure. But you need to know how many 'income units' are represented by that roll. If there is a husband at work, a non-working wife and one 17-year-old, plus another member of the family at college, that is only one unit, but four electoral roll members. It is usually better to divide the income by the 'income units' present at regular worship. The 'giving base' of a church is made up of the 'income units' in the worshipping congregation.

We will not, however, focus on details, important as these are. For the Church Commissioners still deal in vast sums of money and those sums must be handled to good purpose; and even the smallest of dioceses is now having 'million pound' budgets put out to 'the quota' (nor do these sums include the Church Commissioners block grants). The Church of England is thus a multi-million pound organization.

It is the principles we must focus on. They are more important than the details. Yet *church financing seems rarely to be understood*. This is the other quarter of the Church's problem on finance.

The PCC treasurer

'We have a financial problem,' says the PCC treasurer. He is usually wrong. It is not a problem but a symptom! What then is the problem? Here are nine possibilities.

One: most of the discussion to date on the PCC has been about the size of the deficit, and not about the purpose, programme or priorities of the Church. But the PCC members would be more motivated if they were discussing the goals of the church rather than keeping the organization solvent.

Two: there is an absence in the church of agreed specific goals for ministry. The parish is problem-orientated rather than planning-orientated.

Three: there is no systematic biblical teaching on giving — at least once a year (including teaching on tithing!).

Four: the budget is planned by extrapolating from last year's figures. The vicar has not first prayed and discussed with others where the church should be 'growing to' next year.

Five: the pastoral care of the congregation is weak, the evangelism is minimal and the total membership is declining faster than the levels of expenditure.

Six: there is what Schaller describes as

> too much pastor for too few people. The pastor may be suffering more from being under employed rather than from being under paid or under appreciated, but the basic purpose of the Christian Church is not providing employment and satisfactions for clergy.[8]

Seven: the church is being subsidized by the quota. Studies have shown that it is rare to find a congregation that has been receiving financial subsidies for more than three or four years that is also experiencing numerical growth.[9] Self-worth is low when churches are not growing and not paying their way but being subsidized. Besides people are usually more motivated to get involved (and give) in an organization in which they feel they are in control.

Eight: the church is acting as a 'landlord' and as 'provider of space' to numerous outside organizations, and the vicar says 'a lot of activities are now going on in the church.'

Nine: the church is spending more than two-thirds of its income on church staff (e.g. the vicar, via the quota). If it is a 'multiple staff' church, it is spending less than two-thirds on staff (it has not enough staff for the 'ministry out-put').

The chairman of the DBF

'This year we have done very well,' says the chairman of the Diocesan Board of Finance. 'Only a few parishes have not been able to meet the quota. There is a small surplus at the end of the year and the Church Commissioners' subsidy has been proportionately less this year than last year. So it is particularly good. I'm not worried, therefore, over the increase in this year's costs.'

But *can* he be so confident? When should the chairman of the Diocesan Board of Finance begin to be worried? Here are thirteen occasions.

One: when the Diocese does not have an accepted definition of what its function really is. The Canon Missioner talks about the 'mission' of the Church; but he means one thing — political change. Many of those being asked to give to support that mission mean another thing — the conversion of men and women to Jesus Christ.

Two: when the synod members think the primary goal of church funding is to keep the Diocese going and to keep men in the ministry rather than to ensure the growth of the church.

Three: when articulate businessmen, archdeacons, pastoral committees and boards of finance involved in the financial planning of the Diocese know nothing about how churches grow. For beyond a certain figure the only way to increase real income is to increase the membership of the congregations of the parishes.

Four: when there is no budgetary review against the criterion of the growth of the parishes and the diocese.

Five: when those asked to give have not been involved in approving the projects they are asked to support; and when it is assumed that a vote in a synod is all that is required to ensure the necessary finance. (A vote in a synod can mean very little, because the Church is a voluntary, non-profit organization; there are no sanctions, only motivation.)

Six: when it is assumed that small churches can be asked to subsidize other churches that have been in existence for more than five years. This would be to ensure that such small churches divert all their energies to questions of finance and not of the gospel.

Seven: when it is assumed that middle-sized churches can subsidize other churches that have been in existence for more than five years. They can, but to do so would mean they could not employ an extra staff person. But this will be necessary if they are to break through the 'one hundred and fifty' barrier. Furthermore, in an age of unemployment they have a moral responsibility to generate more jobs.

Eight: when it is assumed that certain large churches can subsidize other churches that have been in existence for more than five years. Large churches that have begun to fund their own staff are proportionally as expensive to run as many small churches.

At this point it needs to be said that 'being wealthy' in church financing is determined not by the size of the income, but by what is left over after the necessary expenditure has been made. This is illustrated in a large, growing church. Such a church has a large income because it has a large congregation; and it has a large congregation because it is meeting ministry needs. This involves hiring staff, increasing the building size, spending considerable amounts on communication — the 'life blood' of any organization — and spending money on training.

The 'cheapest' church is the one vicar with a congregation of one hundred and fifty. But if such a church is to grow it will cost the congregation more money — probably by having an extra person on the staff: that could be a curate or a lay person (perhaps an administrator or a secretary). Growth is not cheap: but 'God is no man's debtor'. As we give, so in

God's economy we 'get'.

Nine: when the suggestion in the General Synod Report *How should the Church pay its way?* is ignored. It was suggested there that:

> Most parishes should aim to become financially self-supporting by about 1990. A longer-term aim, to be achieved by about the end of the century, should be that each parish should give away to others £1 for every £1 spent on maintaining the parish [obviously diocesan subsidies should always be available for 'mission' designated areas or projects, urban or rural, but with a time limit].[10]

Ten: when it ignores the possibility of encouraging voluntary inter-church help:

> Financial subsidies coming *directly* from other congregations appear to have less of a negative impact on a new mission than those that come via denominational channels.[11]

Thus, a curate leaves a growing church to become a vicar in another part of the country in a small church. His former parish helps him 'prime the pump' of the new parish by paying a proportion of the salary of a full-time secretary; or a local inner-city parish has a special relationship with a church in the suburbs, and the suburban church 'primes the pump' by paying for a youth worker.

Eleven: when James 4:2 is forgotten: 'You do not have, because you do not ask.' Prayer is essential in financial matters as it is in anything else in the church.

Twelve: when it is forgotten that churches that motivate their members to give probably teach at the same time that people should give to World Mission. The claims of a diocese in a prosperous Western society have, therefore, to compete with the claims of a diocese in the Third World or the claims of a missionary society. The individual Christian will allocate his or her resources in the light of these claims.

Thirteen: when archbishops and bishops are suggesting that the Virgin Birth and the Empty Tomb are optional as doctrine in the Church of England. Nothing demotivates giving as much as fundamental doctrinal confusion in a church.

PART 4

The Future

17

Renewal

It is not exaggerating to say that the future of the Church of England is at stake. Of course, it will continue in *some* form or another. But who really wants mere survival? The question is: will the Church of England be an effective and growing force for Jesus Christ in the nation fifteen years hence?

Cancer in the Church

We have seen that the fundamental problem is doctrinal. Nor, as we have seen, has the Bishop of Durham *caused* these problems over the Virgin Birth and Empty Tomb. He has simply exposed them.

But the strength of the Church of England is that its system has enabled the Church *at last* to face these fundamental questions. For this we can thank synodical government. In the earlier part of the century attempts were made to open up discussion of these controversial issues especially following the Modern Churchmen's Union conference at Girton in 1921. But Randall Davidson, the Archbishop of Canterbury, refused to get drawn into the controversy. The views of the Modernist H. D. A. Major, who denied the Empty Tomb, were referred to him; but he argued that it was a 'diocesan' matter and he didn't want to interfere with the Bishop of Oxford. The controversy was thus confined to the diocesan level.

There were from time to time, as we have seen, debates in

the Convocations. But it had to wait until February 13th 1985 for the question over what *is* the Church of England's teaching on the Virgin Birth and the Empty Tomb to be put officially onto the agenda of the Church of England. That was the date for a debate in the General Synod on the *Nature of Christian Belief*. All the issues that had been lying around (and festering) since 1921 or certainly since 1938 were brought into the open. This time they are having to be resolved.

We have also seen the seriousness of the issues not only in terms of the truth but also in terms of how they work out in the life of the Church.

It was St Paul who argued that false teaching in the Church spreads like a *cancer*. He was referring to certain 'false teachers' in his day who were confusing people about the resurrection of believers. Like a number of teachers in the Church of England today, these people were 'spiritualizing' the Resurrection. And so we read in 2 Timothy 2:17: 'Their talk will eat its way like gangrene [or, literally, cancer].' Cancer starts small. At first there are few symptoms. For a bit you can carry on as normal. But then gradually and terribly the cancer takes over; everything is destroyed and death is the result *unless something is done*. And the earlier you deal with a cancer the easier it is. But whatever stage a cancer has reached, it is always important to deal with it immediately.

There are many who are saying that the Church of England is in a very serious condition because it has 'cancer' — the cancer of false teaching by bishops who are declaring as optional belief in the Virgin Birth and the Empty Tomb. It must therefore be dealt with immediately. Nor is this false teaching over some secondary issue. It is false teaching that touches the heart of Christianity and the heart of the gospel. For St Paul wrote, 'If you confess with your lips that Jesus is Lord and believe in your heart that God raised him from the dead, you will be saved' (Rom 10:9). Paul saw that not *any* belief could be held at the same time as you uttered credal statements.

The basic Creed is: 'Jesus is Lord'. But it is not just *mouthing* the words that is important. It is what you believe and think that is vital. So Paul made it clear that the Christian is someone who believes that God raised Jesus from the dead. And as we have seen in the early Church that meant belief in the Empty Tomb.

Church and nation

But have we got it all wrong? Should we be trying to get a solution to these problems in the Church? Maybe the Church has to experience something of a breakdown!

This seemed to be the view of the Bishop of Durham when he wrote in *Marxism Today* in October 1984. His argument there was that 'it is not until you get breakdowns that you get breakthroughs.'[1] But is that right? Do we really want the Church of England to 'break down'? Surely not. And there are three reasons why.

First, it needs to be said repeatedly that it is easy to break things down. It is not so easy to build them up. Sometimes it may take centuries. Secondly, we should be 'eager to maintain the unity of the Spirit' (Eph 4:3) and there is the serious biblical warning that 'if anyone destroys God's temple, God will destroy him' (1 Cor 3:17). Thirdly, the breakdown of the Church of England would have serious effects on the nation at large. Let me explain.

The Church of England is 'by law established'. This in fact has meant, over the centuries, that the Church is tied in with the state at a number of points. As a consequence the assumptions of public life are still Christian in a general way.

In England there is no written code or constitution on which the nation is founded. In this we are unlike the United States of America, for example. We have an unwritten constitution held together by the Crown as head of state and *governor of the Church of England*. In this way the sovereign symbolizes Christian values as being the official values of the nation. They are thus woven into our English system. But were the Church of England to suffer a serious decline, what values would inform our public life? Presumably the Church would have to be disestablished. You could not have a Church that was clearly a minority Church having special privileges. But this would leave a serious vacuum in society. What would be the standards our society corporately looked to? You could end up with a moral as well as spiritual vacuum. And no society can hold together for long without *some* value system.

Nor is there any such thing as pluralism in a fundamental sense. Let it be said quite clearly that there must be some *agreed* goals. Much of the discussion about pluralism is most misleading. As we have seen, no grouping, large or small, can survive without *some* shared assumptions and goals. Of course, these may include the goal of religious tolerance. But that, we must note, is derived from the Christian view of man as being essentially 'free to choose' — he can accept or reject God for God gives man that right. Indeed, so many liberal values can only be sustained by a Christian world view! There has been the possibility of 'subordinate pluralism' because fundamentally we have been relying on *Christian* values. So were the Church of England seriously to go into a decline, much might be at stake at a social level.

Duties of the Church

As it is, the Church of England has certain duties with regard to the state. But if it could no longer fulfil these obligations in any significant way, public life would suffer more than most imagine. Max Warren once spoke of five duties the Church has towards the state.[2]

First, it must challenge the corruptions of power:

> To a formidable extent we are today ruled by administrative decrees, by means of which power has become impersonalised. It is very difficult to appeal for justice to a bureaucracy.[3]

But because the Church holds certain beliefs about the dignity of man, it will want to champion individual rights against injustices.

Second, the Church is to raise the moral consciousness in the Nation. Warren argues:

It is not for the Church to try to make the Nation good by Act of Parliament. It is for the Church so to influence the conscience of the Nation that acts of Parliament will be passed which forbid what has now come to be recognised as bad, and to facilitate what is newly recognised as good.[4]

Third, the Church is to make people aware that the state is much more than Parliament. The nationalized industries, the National Health Service, the trades unions, the banks, the universities etc are all part of the structures of power. The Church through its members is then to influence these structures for Christ and to achieve his will in them.

Fourth, the Church should identify and meet needs. Max Warren quotes Lord Beveridge, architect of the Welfare State:

The State is or can be a master of money, but in a free society it is master of very little else. The making of a good society depends not on the State but on the citizens acting individually or in free association with one another, acting on motives of various kinds, some selfish, others unselfish, some narrow and material, others inspired by love of man and love of God. The happiness or unhappiness of the society in which we live depends upon ourselves as citizens, not on the instrument of political power which we call the State.[5]

That is why it is so essential for the Church to see evangelism as a social as well as a spiritual duty. Only as men and women are remade by the Holy Spirit of God will these basic social needs be met.

Fifth, the Church is to supply 'meaning' for our society (that was Dean Kelley's point). Warren speaks of:

A state of mind of one who has been pulled up from his moral roots, who has no longer got any moral standards 'but only disconnected urges' who has no longer 'any sense of continuity, of folk, of obligation'.[6]

The role of the Church is to provide fellowship and a sense of purpose in life to people in that condition.

These are functions of all churches in respect of their social responsibility. But the Church of England, as the Established Church, has a special responsibility *and is looked to as having that responsibility.* So if the Church of England declined beyond a certain point, it would have serious consequences for the nation's social health. There is no evidence to date of any other churches being able to fulfil these functions instead of the Church of England.

Renewal of the Church

For these reasons, and above all for the demands of the gospel, we cannot think in terms of anything but church renewal and church growth. The nation needs to see churches growing. And in this ecumenical age it is important to say this: we want to see, on the one hand churches in the main denominations and, on the other hand independent free (Trinitarian) churches growing and becoming the sort of churches Jesus Christ, the head of the Church, wants them to become. Anglicans will rejoice at church growth anywhere and everywhere.

But our focus is the Church of England. We will, therefore, especially be looking to see Anglican churches growing throughout the land. Large churches need to grow larger. Small churches need to grow larger and intermediate-sized churches need to grow larger (and all need to think about sending out 'church planters').

Most churches will not be very large. In the industrialized countries the proportion of large to intermediate and to small churches seems to be the same. So where there is vigorous church growth and a number of very large churches there are proportionately many more intermediate and small churches. In such situations large churches act as a model and stimulus to other churches. It may also be that a spate of church planting stimulates the growth of larger churches. There is some evidence for this.

We have already spoken about 'small church' growth. But more needs to be said about the growth of larger churches, for worldwide alongside the growth of church planting there is also the growth and development of the larger church. In England, there is a dearth of larger churches; the United States has over

300 churches with over 2000 in the congregation. There are none in England. All Souls', Langham Place is probably the largest Anglican Church, with under 2000. These larger churches used to be thought of as typically American. But they are now developing in other parts of the world. Brian Stiller, editor of *Faith Alive,*[7] argues:

> The smaller church is not on the way out and continues to be the ultimate strength of our faith communities. But larger churches are more and more becoming a visible response to the variety of human need . . . [they] provide a social significance that a small church cannot.

There are dangers the large church has to be aware of, as there are in other sized churches. But Brian Stiller says:

> Larger church facilities can handle a number of groups at the same time. More money from a larger congregation underwrites start-up costs for new programmes. And greater resources and an increased staff offer a greater variety of programmes, responding to problems caused by the stress of modern living.

After the priority of establishing new congregations, the next priority is to encourage the growth of larger churches in England. In addition to the reasons given above there are three more.

First, the larger the church, the more likely you are to attract people in the 20 to 40 age group. In fact a survey of (English) Anglican churches indicated that in *all* churches the largest growth area is among this group.[8]

Secondly, the larger the church, the larger the proportion of men in the congregation. This was the finding of the same survey. It also revealed that 77 per cent of the churches had less than 40 per cent of men in the congregation. As the Church of England obviously needs to attract men it seems that it cannot ignore the building-up of larger churches.

Thirdly, although newly planted churches are likely to grow fastest, as a general rule the larger the church, the easier it is to grow. This also the survey confirmed. In a large church the changes that have to accompany numerical expansion are not felt to be disruptive. The variety that is part of the fabric of a large church conditions people to be willing to accept change.

Renewal of worship

But the great test of genuineness in church life is the worship, the prayer life and the fellowship. In the book of Revelation there are cameos of churches which no doubt were well organized and appeared successful; but the judgement of the risen Christ upon them was that they were not all they seemed! One had 'abandoned the love [it] had at first' (2:4); another had 'the name of being alive' but was in reality 'dead' (3:1); yet another was 'neither cold nor hot' — it was just 'lukewarm' (3:16). So today, churches are not necessarily what they seem. But few churches can manufacture a totally false 'worship experience'.

There is renewed interest in worship. Three factors have contributed. First, new forms of worship more appropriate to today's world have been worked out in the Alternative Service Book. There is no doubt a long way to go. But the Alternative Service Book in the Church of England, with all its faults — theological, linguistic and liturgical — has stimulated a freshness of approach in worship and much experiment. Nor is this unAnglican. Cranmer in the Preface to the Book of Common Prayer only opposed what was

> Either of dangerous consequence (as secretly striking at some established Doctrine, or laudable Practice of the Church of England, or indeed of the whole Catholick Church of Christ) or else of no consequence at all, but utterly frivolous and vain.

Experiments in worship in recent years have mostly been in terms of 'idiom' rather than 'content'.

The second factor has been the Evangelical revival we have referred to. In the Anglican Church this has produced a new inventiveness both in terms of music and services. From the mid-sixties onwards, much has been happening. Canon Michael Botting chaired a committee which produced the CPAS Family Service — a format of service that has been used up and down the country. And Bishop Michael Baughen encouraged the writing of new music for songs, choruses and psalms. He had a significant involvement in *Youth Praise* (published in 1966); *Psalm Praise* (1973); and *Hymns for Today's Church* (1982). Much of this work was obviously experimental and not destined to last. But some of it will. This is especially true of the hymns of Bishop Timothy Dudley-Smith.

The third factor in the development of current worship is the charismatic movement. This, too, developed new music and worship forms. There were writers and musicians like Jeanne Harper, the Fisherfolk and the singers of St Michael-le-Belfry. They produced their own brand of music. Somewhat 'middle-class' and 'pretty', it nevertheless fulfilled a need and encouraged others to follow where they pioneered. In fact their experiments led to the most significant of all developments in modern worship (other than the ASB) — the evolution of a new wave of popular Christian music associated with the Bible weeks of the house church movement, certain American Pentecostal groups and some well-known British Christian folk singers. By the time of *Mission England* these songs had gained such currency in many churches and chapels that they formed the staple diet of music on a number of evenings of Billy Graham's mission. The significance of this music is its robust quality. As someone has said: 'It is music that men can sing'. It also has a wider 'class' catchment. It is not particularly middle class. It has now made its way into Anglican churches, and where sensitively used is setting a new dimension to worship. What is common to the new worship forms is that they allow greater play to the emotions — something often neglected in the past.

Doctrine and worship

But worship is not exclusively about forms, styles and emotions — how we feel and how we can express our feelings. For there has to be a balance in worship. Besides the emotions, the mind and the will must be fully employed. Ron Jenson and Jim Stevens describe this balance in these terms:

> The intellectual response minus the emotional and volitional responses equals deadness. It creates an academic approach to God.

The emotional response minus the intellectual and volitional responses equals feelings for feelings' sake, void of a meaningful tie to
the gospel's content. This leads to excess. If the volitional response
is emphasised more than the other two, the result will be an unhealthy introspection and feeling of perpetual guilt.[9]

But once we talk about the intellectual dimension of worship
we are back into fundamental doctrine. For worship is to come
to God *as he is*. It involves 'waiting' on God. The Psalmist
described his worship experience as 'I waited patiently for the
Lord' (Ps 40:1). He was depressed or in trouble. But after his
'waiting' the Lord came to him and 'put a new song in [his]
mouth, a song of praise' (v.3). But 'to wait does not mean to sit
for hours in a yoga position with eyes shut and with the mind
neutral,' say Jenson and Stevens.

> It does mean focusing, quietly and reflectively on God. It neces-
> sitates disengaging the mind from the cares, frustration, and
> activities of our frantic lifestyle, and engaging the mind in
> thoughtful reflection on God.[10]

But this God we worship is the God who is revealed pre-
eminently in his word (in Scripture). But if certain bishops
are confusing some of the faithful in their understanding of
God, worship will become for them little more than enter-
tainment or an aesthetic event. They will not be able to focus
on God as he really is. And without true worship individuals
and churches cease to grow.

But confusion over doctrine does not only destroy worship,
it also destroys faith and prayer. Our faith in God depends on
what we know about him. Our prayers are directly related to
our faith. For example, if I cannot believe that God intervenes
and acts in respect of the details of life in answer to prayer,
then obviously I won't pray about these details.

Prayer

In his Easter Letter for 1985 the Archbishop of York seemed
to suggest it was odd that a clergyman should admit on a television programme that God was interested in getting him a

parking space when he needed it (and prayed). But the alternative to believing specific prayer is so vague ('when many people are praying . . . the atmosphere gets sensitized,' to quote the Archbishop of York on the same television programme[11]).

In a similar vein the Bishop of Durham seems to deny that God would intervene miraculously to heal. He was being interviewed by John Mortimer for the *Sunday Times*.[12] In response to a question about God arranging 'a miraculous resurrection of the body [of Jesus] and the release from the tomb' he said this:

> Although he *could* have done it, it doesn't seem to be the way he goes about things. But the real point is that concentrating on the miraculous sidetracks people. *It encourages them to believe in all sorts of other things like spiritual healing* [italics mine].

But if the Bishop cannot believe that God intervenes like this, he won't pray for him to do so. The principle is this: if you cannot believe that God intervenes in the details of life, naturally you won't pray for his intervention. This teaching, of course, seems to run contrary to the teaching of Jesus in the Sermon on the Mount who says 'Ask, and it shall be given you; seek, and you will find; knock, and it will be opened to you' (Mt 7:7).

It would seem wrong, therefore, to discourage faith in the 'God . . . who gives life to the dead and calls into existence the things that do not exist' (Rom 4:17). For at the same time people who do this are discouraging 'believing prayer'. And both faith in God and believing prayer are essentials for the growth of the Church.

Leonard Hodgson in his Gifford lectures put the Christian position on petitionary prayer very well:

> If in other directions God puts the doing of his will on earth into our hands, and lets it wait upon our doing our duty, why should we be surprised if he works in the same manner in the matter of prayer? . . . To believe that often he does not act until we ask him, is not the mark of a foolish, a childish, faith. It is the consciousness of growing manhood on the part of the creature, the recognition that God has laid on him the responsibility of deciding whether *in this detail* the divine creative purpose shall go forward or be delayed.

18

Facing the facts

Two challenges

As the Church of England faces the future, there are two challenges that can't be ignored.

In the first place there is a challenge from David Watson. Not long before he died, he wrote these words:

> When ordained clergymen openly . . . reject the bodily resurrection of Christ, clear discipline needs to be taken. Given the need for compassion when any Christian, including a leader, is wrestling with honest doubts on even most basic doctrines, *we need also the courage to stop such a theologian or teacher from exercising a public ministry whilst working through their personal uncertainties.* The Roman Catholic church has often shown here the discipline that other churches have lacked.[1] (Italics mine.)

In the second place, and from a totally different position, there has been a challenge from Peter Baelz, the Dean of Durham. He has called for 'public clarification' over 'the question of what Anglicans count as orthodoxy'. In a letter to *The Times*[2] he supported

> the essential orthodoxy of those who confess the truth of the Incarnation but are unable to affirm *ex animo* the historicity of the stories of Jesus's birth as well as of those who confess the truth of the Resurrection but are unable to affirm the historicity of the stories of the empty tomb.

But he went on to write this:

Whether I am right or wrong in my belief, this is a matter which seems to call for public clarification not least because of present conversations between Anglicans and others on the nature of authority in the Church.

Practical problems

The major responsibility rests with the Archbishop of Canterbury. He will have to take the initiative, and in so doing he will first have to address the question, 'What is the teaching of the Church of England on the Virgin Birth and the Empty Tomb?' This question must be addressed quite separately from the question of 'What is the Church of England to do with any bishops who preach and teach contrary to that teaching?' It is essential that the former question is answered with integrity and without reference to the enormous difficulties (both practical and pastoral) inherent in the latter.

But there must be answers. For in addition to ecumenical problems there are at least five serious practical problems that can only be resolved after these questions are answered.

The first practical problem is over confirmation. There have already been requests to certain bishops not to take confirmations until these doctrinal issues are sorted out. Michael Wilcock, the vicar of probably the largest and liveliest congregation in Durham, spoke of the problem in a letter to the *Church Times* (March 29th 1985). He said that if the Bishop of Durham had come for a confirmation it

> would have caused a painful split in our congregation . . . At the moment of writing certain questions remain unresolved: notably, whether in the official teaching of the Church of England such doctrines as the virginal conception and bodily resurrection of our Lord are to be regarded as optional or as obligatory. These questions will not simply 'evaporate'. We appreciate Dr. Jenkins's willingness not to come this year for a confirmation at which Bishop and candidates would differ as to the faith that was actually being confirmed. But the same questions will still be there next year if nothing is done about them in the meantime. Our hope for the proposed moratorium is not that by 1986 the whole issue will have stolen away. It is that these matters will be grappled with, and (as I am

sure our Bishop would himself agree) that minds will change. What we look for is resolution, not evaporation.

The second practical problem is that clergy have a very real *moral* dilemma. For many years clergy have tolerated heretical leaders under the teaching of Article XXVI *Of the Unworthiness of the Ministers which hinders not the effect of the Sacrament:*

> Sometimes the evil have chief authority in the Ministration of the Word and Sacraments, yet forasmuch as they do not the same in their own name, but in Christ's, and do minister by his commission and authority, *we may use* their Ministry, both in hearing the Word of God, and in receiving of the Sacraments.

Being Anglican no one wishes to act prematurely. So this has been the grounds for inaction. But now many clergy are saying that 'enough is enough'. First, they know that this Article was not written to encourage them to tolerate *indefinitely* men who are heretical: rather it was written to remind them that the Church of Christ is bigger than such ministers. We may have bishops (even archbishops) declaring optional fundamental doctrines of the faith — but the Church's doctrine does not depend on such episcopal pronouncements, but on the mind of Christ as revealed by his Holy Spirit in Scripture and confirmed by the Church as a whole. And ministry is 'by his commission and authority'.

Secondly, it was written to help those consciences that were worried about receiving invalid sacraments from these men. But their worries were unfounded. They should realize, so the Article implies, that their baptism was Christian because these men were ministering on behalf of the whole Church of Christ even though they might be very wrong themselves! It is Christ's sacrament — not the private possession of any individual. For that reason, it was said, they may use their ministry. The Article never (in the Latin or English) said they *must* use their ministry!

And the Article was balanced; for having ruled out the early heresy of Donatism (a sort of requirement for clerical perfectionism) it then *demanded* action:

> Nevertheless it appertaineth to the discipline of the Church, that

inquiry be made of evil Ministers, and that they be accused by those that have knowledge of their offences: and finally being found guilty, by just judgement be deposed.

Dilemmas for the clergy

The dilemma for the clergy is how to achieve this discipline. The official method is to use the law and go to court under *The Ecclesiastical Jurisdiction Measure 1963*. But for many there is an instinctive reaction against heresy trials. English history does not encourage us to think that this is necessarily a productive way forwards!

So what should such clergy do? All they can do is exert 'pressure', but that has not been very productive either. It was not able to persuade the Archbishop of York to defer the consecration of David Jenkins. That is why the Church of England *must* resolve these present problems. For if 'pressure' builds up beyond a certain point there is bound to be an explosion!

A third practical problem facing the Church relates to another dilemma the clergy have. In the case of a 'doubting bishop' they are in a situation of 'canonical obedience' under a man who is forfeiting his right to this obedience. For 'canonical obedience' to a bishop is never absolute. It is qualified.

In the Book of Common Prayer it is described as a submission to 'their *godly* admonitions, and . . . their *godly* judgements' (The Ordering of Priests). It is not *any* admonition or judgement that has to be submitted to, only what is 'godly'. In the Alternative Service Book the phrase is 'Will you . . . give *due* respect to those in authority?' So obedience is never an absolute ('I will pay true and canonical obedience to the Lord Bishop . . . in all things *lawful* and *honest*' — cf. Canon C.14). 'Lawful' (i.e. according to the Canons) is the first qualifier. 'Honest' is next; then comes 'godly' (from the Book of Common Prayer). The word 'due' of the ASB is meant as shorthand for all these qualifiers. So when his bishop's teaching is technically 'unlawful' (because it is uncanonical), 'dishonest' (because it is untrue) and 'ungodly' (because it leads people away from Christ), how does the parochial clergyman respond? The Ordinal implies that he should *not* submit to *'ungodly* admonitions and judgements'.

His dilemma is compounded by the fact that he *himself* is under a legal as well as a moral and spiritual duty 'to banish and drive away all erroneous and strange doctrines contrary to God's Word'. This is the requirement of the priest in the 1662 Ordinal (the 'shorthand' in the new Ordinal is the duty 'to uphold the truth of the gospel against error'). So the clergyman himself has a canonical duty to prevent erroneous doctrines from gaining currency.

Completing the agenda

But there are further difficulties beyond problems over confirmations and easing the consciences of the clergy. The fourth practical problem facing the Church relates to ACCM (The Advisory Council for the Church's Ministry).

The doctrinal confusion in the Church of England presents problems on two fronts as far as ACCM is concerned. First, there is the perception of the Church of England's ministry (from a doctrinal point of view) as it is seen by potential ordinands. Young men with vision, drive and an assured faith are not going to be attracted by bishops denying essential elements of that faith.

But, secondly, there is the question of what sort of faith the Church of England is looking for in its ordinands. When ACCM was establishing criteria for selection, the criteria suggested seemed to prejudice a person of conviction! For in an ACCM paper in June 1983 *(Selection for Ministry: a Report on Criteria)* it was suggested that selectors should prefer a man whose faith is 'an active search for fuller insight; a restless quest for truth'. Its view was that 'certainty is therefore not to be had . . . and firmness is to be found, we suggest, not so much in credal statements'. But this doesn't seem to bear much of a relationship with Canon A.5. If ever ACCM were to reject good men of conviction *because of their convictions* that would be very serious indeed. Perhaps it should be said that a criterior of selection for ministry in 2 Timothy 2:2, is that of 'having faith' — not 'having doubts'!

But the fifth practical problem caused by the current doctrinal confusion in the Church of England relates to the General Synod's agenda.

Currently before the Church there are matters of the greatest importance as far as its membership is concerned. I refer to marriage and divorce, the ministry of women in the Church, ecumenical relationships, nuclear disarmament and matters relating to 'personal origins' (embryo research, abortion etc). None of these issues is clear cut (which doesn't mean to say we cannot have clear-cut policies over them). All would agree that we are dealing in shades of grey; for some, the grey is just 'off white'; but all admit there is *something* to discuss. But if as a Church we cannot agree over fundamentals there is no way we can get useful discussion on what, in fact, are subordinate issues.

If the Church of England comes, through its bishops, to a full reaffirmation of historical Christianity, with a commitment to belief in the Virgin Birth and the Empty Tomb, it will not lead to a monochrome church of robotic believers. There will still be much disagreement over various topics. But it will be disagreement among Christians who are agreed over fundamentals. This is precisely as we would expect. New knowledge and technology and new forms of social organization generate new problems never before imagined. But when a church is agreed over fundamentals, it can stage a genuine (even if heated) discussion and there can be attempts at problem solving.

But when a church is not agreed over fundamentals, all that is possible is for the 'entrenched positions' to play politics. For example, those who have decided that women should be ordained priests engineer their positions. Those who have decided that women should not be ordained priests engineer their positions. There is hardly an attempt to discuss the theological questions. Politics is the only option left! But this is not the way a church should do its business. The Church should be discussing *theologically* all these crucial issues.

John Wycliffe

The Church of England has problems and possibilities. At the beginning of this book we referred to 1984 as being the year of the death of David Watson, the consecration of David Jenkins and Billy Graham's *Mission England*. We have also mentioned Lesslie Newbigin in connection with that year. But 1984 also saw the 600th anniversary of the death of John Wycliffe. He was an amazing man; he was rugged, sometimes fierce, often political and, according to G. M. Trevelyan, 'with certain want of attractiveness, owing to the predominance of hard intellectual and moral qualities over the emotions'[3]; but he was a great reformer of the Church of England. So he now has his own place in the Anglican lectionary, when he is remembered as 'Theologian, Reformer' on December 31st. For on that day he died, in his mid-fifties, celebrating Holy Communion in his Parish Church of Lutterworth.

But what lessons has he for us today in the Church of England as we face the future?

The world of the twentieth century is so different from the world of the fourteenth. The best picture of life in those days comes from Chaucer in the *Canterbury Tales* and William Langland in *Piers Plowman*. It is clear from them that the Church also is now so different. But we have this in common: the official Church was failing to commend the gospel of Christ to the world; the clergy, or many of them, were failing in their leadership of the church; and individual Christians were being spiritually starved.

Wycliffe was in no doubt about what should be done:

> The office of a Christian, to which the faithful should diligently attend, ought to be twofold: to purge the Church Militant of false shoots not bedded in the highest Pastor, who is the vine of the entire Church; and to dispose its branches that they may better bear fruit for the blessing of the Church.[4]

So begins his treatise *On the Pastoral Office*.

The Church needed purging and reorganizing, but above all the clergy needed to preach the word of God. They were not there to collect money, or even celebrate the mass. For 'there are two things that pertain to the status of pastor: the holiness of the pastor and the wholesomeness of his teaching.'[5] For this reason Wycliffe says that the first duty of the pastor is 'to cleanse his own spring, that it may not infect the word of God.'[6]

The pastoral office was threefold according to Wycliffe:

> First [he is] to feed his sheep spiritually on the word of God, that through pastures ever green they may be initiated into the blessedness of heaven. The second pastoral office is to purge wisely the sheep of disease, that they may not infect themselves and others as well. And the third is for the pastor to defend his sheep from ravening wolves, both sensible and insensible.[7]

Wycliffe's strategy

But how did Wycliffe actually achieve his goals? He taught, he translated and he organized. By 1390 he was the Master of Balliol College, Oxford. Indeed, he was a leading figure in the University at a time when Oxford had become the most important university in Europe. His students absorbed his ideas. But he realized that the greatest priority was for the Bible to be translated into English. Only a minority of the population knew Latin. The Bible had to be available for all. So this is the origin of Wycliffe's Bible, the first Bible in English. Parts had been translated before, but mainly for special uses — no one had translated it from Genesis to Revelation. The translations (there were two versions) probably were done by Wycliffe's disciples, for he was a great delegater.

When the Bible was translated, he had to spread the word. But how? There were no printing presses yet. Few men could read. So his followers went round the country preaching and reading the Bible. They were not always bothered about the existing church organization. If there was a place where the word of God was not being preached, in they would go. They would preach in barns, fields, homes as well as churches. Some may have been overenthusiastic, but the claims of the gospel were more pressing than the niceties of Church organization.

Indeed, Wycliffe taught that when a church was being corrupted by false teachers, the people in the pews should use financial sanctions. He advocated the non-payment of tithes in such cases:

> When a curate is notoriously negligent in his pastoral office, they as subjects, yea, ought to withdraw offerings and tithes from him and whatever might offer occasion for the fostering of such wickedness . . . Such people sustaining a curate thus notoriously give alms imprudently against Christ. No one should do this; therefore people should not support such a curate with alms. For Christ commands, 'Beware of false prophets who come to you in the clothing of sheep, yet inwardly are ravenous wolves![8]

But Wycliffe never left the Church. He simply taught and acted. Does he suggest a strategy for today's church?

A contemporary strategy

First, one thing must be said to those Anglicans who feel misled by some in the current leadership of the Church: there should certainly not be an exodus to other churches. Article XXVI reminds us that the Church is more than individual leaders who may be in error. And the Church of England has a great potential future. We could be on the verge of a significant spiritual awakening. The time is ripe. The Enlightenment age is nearly over. Around the world an age enlightened by the gospel seems to be dawning.

However, if the leadership and the synodical structures fail to reform the Church of England, the people and clergy of the Church of England cannot sit back for ever. They all have a duty to both God and the nation.

The urgency of the situation is seen when we are specific. For example at present on Tyneside at least 93 per cent of the population are not in church on a given Sunday. And only 2 per cent will be in Anglican churches. Figures nationwide are only slightly better. Something has to be done. The people of England need to hear the gospel. 'But how are men to call upon him in whom they have not believed? And how are they to believe in him of whom they have never heard? And how are they to hear without a preacher? And how can men preach unless they are sent?' (Rom 10:14-15).

We could suggest a Wycliffite strategy for the present that would have four essentials. First, there should be the component of adequate *Christian* (not *sub-Christian*) theological teaching and research. The apostolic Church must out-think those who would oppose it or subvert it. Secondly, there should be the component of 'liberating the Bible for common use'. In twentieth-century terms this will require among other things the Church to have *better access to broadcasting*. After all it is intolerable that at present decisions about religious broadcasting should so often be in the hands of those outside the Church. The third component should be for 'preachers' to be 'out among the people'. In twentieth-century terms these will at least include 'church planters'. The fourth component, if we follow Wycliffe, should be the use of financial sanctions to reform the Church! He would seem to be arguing that people should not give money indefinitely towards activities, policies and people that are destructive of the Church. This is especially so when there are many first rate Christian causes crying out for their giving but which are currently being starved of resources.

The fire at York

The Church in the nation is at a crossroads. And there are two final questions we must ask. Can the Church of England be revived *as a whole?* At present many Anglican churches that are committed to the apostolic gospel and present it in a contemporary style are seeing remarkable growth. But will others follow their lead? This is question number one.

Question number two is very serious: is the Church of England under judgement? Was what happened in the early hours of Monday morning July 9th 1984 *just* freak lightning?

That was the occasion when the south transept of York Minster caught fire three days after the Archbishop of York had consecrated a man as Bishop in the Church of God who publicly had denied the Virgin Birth of Jesus Christ and cast doubt on his Empty Tomb.

'I've never seen anything like it before. There was no rain or thunder. The flashes got brighter and brighter. And they seemed to last far longer than normal lightning would,' one eye-witness is reported as saying. Mr Stanley Phillips, the deputy fire officer for North Yorkshire, confirmed that the fire which caused £3 million worth of damage *was* caused by lightning. The conclusion of Mr C. G. Collier of the Meteorological Office Radar Research Laboratory was that the rainfall cell that had developed suddenly over York at the time was 'really a heavy shower rather than a thunderstorm. It is surprising that it apparently produced such devastating lightning.'[9]

Is it so wrong, as the Archbishop of York suggested it was, to connect the fire 'with some remarks made by a bishop elect on a TV discussion programme'?[10] Is it so irrational to say that while much suffering is not due to sin, some is? A previous Archbishop of York (and then Archbishop of Canterbury), William Temple, would have thought it perfectly right to make the connection. For thousands of Christians around the world had been praying for the Church of and in England. And William Temple said: 'When I pray coincidences happen; when I cease to pray coincidences cease!'

But let me close with some words of a previous Bishop of Durham, and also a previous Archbishop of York (and then Archbishop of Canterbury), Michael Ramsey. He certainly believes that God's judgement 'through catastrophes' is a real possibility. Speaking of national judgement he said this:

When men and nations turn away from God's laws and prefer the courses dictated by pride and selfishness to the courses dictated by conscience, calamitous results follow. God . . . is present in judgement through catastrophes which follow human willfulness . . . [But] as the judgement of God is accepted and felt, so in the same moment may his lovingkindness and mercy be found . . . Let it however be remembered 'judgement begins at the house of God' (1 Peter 4:17). The Church shows the message of divine judgement to the world as she sees the judgement upon herself and begins to mend her ways.[11]

Notes

Introduction

1. George Orwell, *Nineteen Eighty-Four* (Penguin Books, London, 1954), p.171.
2. July 12th 1984.

Part 1 — Setting the Scene

Chapter 1: 1984 and All That

1. David Watson, *Discipleship* (Hodder and Stoughton, London, 1981).
2. John A.T. Robinson, *Honest to God* (SCM Press, London, 1963).
3. David Watson, *In Search of God* (Falcon, London, 1974).

Chapter 2: Decline and Growth

1. David Barrett, *World Christian Encyclopedia* (Oxford University Press, 1982); other statistics from the Missions Advanced Research and Communication Centre, Monrovia, California.
2. Stephen Neill, *A History of Christian Missions* (Penguin Books, London, 1964), p.559.
3. *Church Statistics — some facts and figures about the Church of England, 1984 edition* (CIO Publishing, London, 1984), p.22.
4. *UK Christian Handbook 1985/86 Edition,* ed. Peter Brierley (MARC Europe, the Evangelical Alliance and the Bible Society, London, 1984), p.111.
5. figures in Stephen Neill, *Anglicanism* (Penguin Books, London, 1960), p.261ff.
6. *Prospects for the Eighties* (Bible Society, London, 1980), p.23.
7. quoted in Dean M. Kelley, *Why Conservative Churches are Growing* (Harper and Row, San Francisco, 1972), p.55.
8. Donald McGavran and George C. Hunter III, *Church Growth — strategies that work* (Abingdon, Nashville, 1980), p.107.
9. Kelley, op. cit.
10. ibid., p.44.

11. ibid., p.134.
12. ibid., p.136.
13. Howard Snyder, *Liberating the Church* (Marshall, Morgan and Scott, Basingstoke, 1983), p.11.
14. quoted in A.R. Vidler, *The Orb and the Cross* (SPCK, London, 1945), p.95.
15. James D. Anderson and Ezra Earl Jones, *The Management of Ministry* (Harper and Row, San Francisco, 1978), p.23.

Part 2 — Doctrinal Arguments

Chapter 3: What Does the Church of England Believe?

1. Stephen Neill, *Anglicanism*, op. cit., p.418.
2. ibid., p.119.
3. ibid., p.132.
4. Richard Hooker, *Of the Laws of Ecclesiastical Policy*, Book III, (1) 5.
5. *The Lambeth Conference 1968, Resolutions and Reports* (SPCK, London), p.140.
6. in H. Bettenson, *Documents of the Christian Church* (Oxford University Press, 1943), p.440.
7. quoted in Stephen Neill, *Anglicanism,* op. cit., p.260.
8. *The Canons of the Church of England* (CIO Publishing, London, 1977).

Chapter 4: Today's World and the Virgin Birth

1. Christopher Booker, *The Neophiliacs* (Collins, London, 1969), p.53.
2. Lucretius, *The Nature of the Universe,* tr. R. E. Latham (Penguin Books, London, 1951), p.29.
3. Basil of Cappadocia, *Hexaemeron,* Homily 1.2.
4. John R. W. Stott in *All Souls — November/December 1984* (All Souls' Church, Langham Place, London).
5. Raymond E. Brown, *The Virginal Conception and the Bodily Resurrection of Jesus* (Geoffrey Chapman, London, 1974), p.52ff.
6. Alan Richardson, *A Dictionary of Christian Theology* (SCM Press, London, 1969), p.357.

Chapter 5: Symbolism and the Empty Tomb

1. David Brown, *The Divine Trinity* (Duckworth, London, 1985), p.5.
2. Ignatius, *To the Ephesians,* 19.
3. Justin, *First Apology*, 21.
4. Ambrose, *De institutione virginis,* 5.36.
5. see the texts in H. Von Campenhausen, *The Virgin Birth in the Theology of the Ancient Church* (SCM Press, London, 1964), p.74ff.
6. F. F. Bruce, *1 and 2 Corinthians* (Marshall, Morgan and Scott, London, 1971), p.139.
7. John Polkinghorne, *The Way the World is* (SPCK, London 1983), p.86.

Chapter 6: The Beginnings of Subversion

1. see J. M. Creed and J. S. Boys Smith, *Religious thought in the Eighteenth Century* (Cambridge University Press, 1934) for a selection of texts from this period including some of Joseph Butler.
2. E. L. Mascall, *The Christian Universe — the Boyle lectures 1965* (Darton, Longman and Todd, London, 1966), p.9.
3. quoted in Robert E. Sullivan, *John Toland and the Deist Controversy* (Harvard University Press, 1982), p.206.
4. Norman Sykes, *The English Religious Tradition* (SCM Press, London, 1961), p.65.
5. quoted in Stephen Neill, *Anglicanism*, op. cit., p.187.
6. John Wesley, *Journal* (Dent Edition), vol.3, p.329.
7. ibid., vol.1, p.102.
8. G. R. Cragg, *The Church and the Age of Reason 1648—1789* (Penguin Books, London, 1960), p.145.
9. William Wilberforce, *A Practical View* (SCM Press, London, 1958), p.14ff.
10. quoted in Stephen Neill, *Anglicanism*, op. cit., p.240.
11. J. F. Bethune-Baker, *The Way of Modernism and other Essays* (Cambridge University Press, 1927), p.2.
12. Alan M. G. Stephenson, *The Rise and Decline of English Modernism* (SPCK, London, 1984), p.7ff.
13. Bethune-Baker, op. cit., p.9.
14. ibid., p.13.

Chapter 7: Modernism and the Bible

1. R. H. Lightfoot, *History and Interpretation in the Gospels* (Hodder and Stoughton, London, 1935), p.225.
2. Bethune-Baker, op. cit., p.15.
3. quoted in F. F. Bruce, *Tradition Old and New* (Paternoster Press, Exeter, 1970), p.40ff.
4. D. E. Nineham and others, *History and Chronology in the New Testament* (SPCK, London, 1965), p.4.
5. R. T. France, *History, Criticism and Faith*, ed. Colin Brown (Inter-Varsity Press, Leicester, 1976), p.106.
6. Basil Willey, *The Seventeenth Century Background* (Chatto and Windus, London, 1934), p.10ff.
7. Bethune-Baker, op. cit., p.14.
8. Stephen Toulmin, *Metaphysical Beliefs* (SCM Press, London, 1970), pp.3-71.
9. Karl Barth, 'Evangelical Theology in the 19th Century', *Scottish Journal of Theology Occasional Papers 8* (Oliver and Boyd, Edinburgh, 1959), p.58.
10. Helmut Thielicke, *A little exercise for young theologians* (Eerdmans, Grand Rapids, 1962), p.33.
11. Handley Moule, *Charles Simeon* (Inter-Varsity Press, London, 1948), p.79.

Chapter 8: The Beginnings of Conversion

1. D. E. Nineham, 'Ye Have Not Passed This Way Heretofore' (Joshua 3:4),

Theology, vol. lxxvii (September 1984), p.364.

2. quoted in Michael Green (ed.), *The Truth of God Incarnate* (Hodder and Stoughton, London, 1977), p.122.

3. R. C. Zaehner, *Drugs, Mysticism and Make-Believe* (Collins, London, 1972), p.39.

4. quoted in Lesslie Newbigin, *The Other Side of 1984* (World Council of Churches, Geneva, 1984), p.7ff.

5. Henry Chadwick, *Lessing's Theological Writings* (A. and C. Black, London, 1956), p.51ff.

6. ibid., p.31.

7. Michael Polanyi, *Personal Knowledge* (Routledge and Kegan Paul, London, 1958), p.266.

8. Newbigin, op. cit., p.63.

9. Martin Esslin (ed.) *Absurd Drama* (Penguin Books, London, 1965), p.13.

10. Theodore Roszak, *The Making of a Counter Culture* (Faber and Faber, London, 1968), p.145ff.

Chapter 9: Crisis in the Church of England

1. Newbigin, op. cit., p.22.

2. ibid., p.23.

3. C. S. Lewis, *God in the Dock* (Collins, London, 1979), p.56.

4. G. H. K. Bell, *Randall Davidson* (Oxford University Press, 1952), p.1137.

5. ibid., p.1144.

6. ibid., p.1144.

7. ibid., p.1145.

8. ibid., p.1145.

9. ibid., p.1150.

10. *York Journal of Convocation*, (2nd/3rd June, 1938), p.30ff.

11. ibid., p.104.

12. ibid., p.128ff.

Chapter 10: The 1938 Doctrine Report

1. June 23rd 1984; full text published as a Diocesan Booklet (Church House, Newcastle, 1984).

2. *York Journal of Convocation* (18th/19th January, 1939), p.54ff.

3. *Doctrine in the Church of England* (SPCK, London, 1938), p.19.

4. ibid., p.3.

5. ibid., p.3.

6. ibid., p.82.

7. ibid., p.84.

8. *York Journal of Convocation* (18th/19th January, 1939), p.55.

9. *Doctrine in the Church of England*, op. cit., p.12.

10. ibid., p.2.

11. *York Journal of Convocation* (2nd/3rd June, 1938), p.9.

12. *York Journal of Convocation* (18th/19th January 1939), p.10.

13. quoted in Bishop Burge's letter to the Archbishop of Canterbury; Bell, op.

cit., p.1148.
14. Paul A. Welsby, *The History of the Church of England 1945–1980* (Oxford University Press, 1984), p.41.
15. Stephenson, op. cit., p.188.
16. J. A. T. Robinson, 'The Resurrection in the NT', *Interpreter's Bible Dictionary*, vol.4 (Abingdon, Nashville, 1962), p.45ff.
17. *Christian Believing* (SPCK, London, 1976).
18. John Hick (ed.), *The Myth of God Incarnate* (SCM Press, London, 1977).
19. *Believing in the Church* (SPCK, London, 1981).

Chapter 11: Current Leadership

1. Dennis Nineham, 'Jesus in the Gospels', in *Christ for Us Today,* ed. Norman Pittenger, (SCM Press, London, 1968), p.64.
2. Stephenson, op. cit., p.197.
3. quoted in Nicholas Lash, *Theology on Dover Beach* (Darton, Longman and Todd, London, 1979), p.120.
4. ibid., p.197.
5. H. W. Montefiore, 'Jesus, the Revelation of God' in Pittenger (ed.), op. cit., p.109.
6. J. D. Douglas (ed.), *Let the Earth Hear His Voice* (World Wide Publications, Minneapolis, 1975).
7. Murray J. Harris, *Easter in Durham — Bishop Jenkins and the Resurrection of Jesus* (Paternoster Press, Exeter, 1985), p.14.
8. ibid., p.16.
9. Booker, op. cit., p.98.

Part 3 — Practical Problems and Possibilities

Chapter 12: Leadership for Growth — Basic Perspectives

1. C. Peter Wagner, *Leading Your Church to Growth* (GL Publications, Ventura, 1984), p.50.
2. Lee Lebsack, *Ten at the Top: How Ten of America's Largest Assemblies of God Churches Grew* (Baker Book House, Grand Rapids, 1974), p.115.
3. Wagner, op. cit., p.58.
4. ibid., p.62.
5. Richard Baxter, *The Reformed Pastor* (SCM Press, London, 1956), p.77.

Chapter 13: Leadership for Growth — Simple Essentials

1. Paul Y. Cho, *Prayer: Key to Revival* (Word (UK), Berkhamsted, 1984), p.10.
2. Ron Jenson and Jim Stevens, *Dynamics of Church Growth* (Baker Book House, Grand Rapids, 1981), p.27.
3. E. M. Blaiklock, *St Luke* (Scripture Union, London, 1966), p.43.
4. George Adam Smith, 'The Book of Isaiah' in *The Expositor's Bible* vol.3 (Eerdmans, Grand Rapids, 1956), p.673.
5. Tina Tietjen, *The Unorganised Manager* (Video Arts, London, 1983), p.12.

6. Ted W. Engstrom and Edward R. Dayton, *The Art of Management for Christian Leaders* (Word Books, Waco, 1976), p.143.

7. John R. W. Stott, *One People* (Falcon, London, 1968), p.66.

8. Ted W. Engstrom, *The Making of a Christian Leader* (Zondervan, Grand Rapids, 1976), p.174.

9. *Video Arts Limited,* Dumbarton House, 68 Oxford Street, London W1N 9LA (01-637 7288).

10. David H. Womack, *The Pyramid Principle* (Bethany Fellowship, Minneapolis, 1977), p.79.

11. Jenson and Stevens, op. cit., p.112.

12. Anderson and Jones, op.cit., p.154.

Chapter 14: Enabling Structures?

1. Douglas W. Johnson, *The Care and Feeding of Volunteers* (Abingdon, Nashville, 1978), p.112.

2. John Tiller, *A Strategy for the Church's Ministry* (CIO Publishing, London, 1983).

3. *Administry* — the inter-church organisation project: 28, Fontwell Close, St Albans, Herts AL3 5HW.

4. Lyle E. Schaller, *Growing Plans* (Abingdon, Nashville, 1983), p.163.

5. *Homosexual Relationships* — *a contribution to discussion* (CIO Publishing, London, 1979), p.52.

6. ibid., p.4.

7. ibid., p.88.

Chapter 15: Geared for Growth

1. Schaller, op. cit., p.21.

2. ibid., p.21.

3. McGavran and Hunter, op. cit., p.83.

4. Carl S. Dudley, *Making the Small Church Effective* (Abingdon, Nashville, 1978), p.49.

5. Schaller, op. cit., p.23.

6. McGavran and Hunter, op. cit., p.93.

7. ibid., p.34.

8. ibid., p.35.

Chapter 16: Church Planting and Finance

1. Michael Marshall, *The Anglican Church Today and Tomorrow* (A. R. Mowbray, Oxford, 1984), p.151.

2. ibid., p.152.

3. ibid., p.153.

4. McGavran and Hunter, op. cit., p.99ff.

5. quoted in ibid., p.100.

6. ibid., p.107.

7. Schaller, op. cit., p.137.

8. Lyle E. Schaller, *Effective Church Planning* (Abingdon, Nashville, 1979),

p.118.
9. Schaller, *Growing Plans,* op. cit., p.142.
10. *How should the Church pay its way?* (Central Board of Finance of the Church of England, 1980), p.10.
11. Schaller, *Growing Plans*, op. cit., p.142.

Part 4 — The Future

Chapter 17: Renewal

1. *Marxism Today*, October 1984, p.27.
2. Max Warren and Raymond Johnson, *The Functions of a National Church* (Latimer House, Oxford, 1984), p.25ff.
3. ibid., p.26.
4. ibid., p.27.
5. Lord Beveridge, *Voluntary Action — A Report on Methods of Social Advance* (Allen and Unwin, London, 1948), p.320.
6. Warren and Johnson, op. cit., p.29.
7. Reported by Michael McAteer, *The Toronto Star,* March 30th 1985.
8. CPAS Policy Group Survey, December 1984.
9. Jenson and Stevens, op. cit., p.37.
10. ibid., p.35.
11. London Weekend Television's *Credo,* February 23rd 1985.
12. *The Sunday Times Review,* May 12th 1985.

Chapter 18: Facing the Facts

1. Watson, *Discipleship*, op. cit., p.67.
2. May 23rd 1984.
3. quoted in Edwin Robertson, *Wycliffe* (Marshall, Morgan and Scott, Basingstoke, 1984), p.9.
4. Text in Library of Christian Classics, vol. xiv, *Advocates of Reform,* ed. Matthew Spinka (SCM, London, 1953), p.32.
5. ibid., p.32.
6. ibid., p.48.
7. ibid., p.48.
8. ibid., p.38.
9. C. G. Collier, *Weather,* vol. 39 (10) October 1984, p.326-7.
10. Letter to *The Times*, July 12th 1984.
11. Michael Ramsey, *The Christian Priest Today* (SPCK, London, 1972), p.22ff.

Appendix 1

The Position

of the North East (Durham and Newcastle) Diocesan Evangelical Fellowship, voted on Monday 3rd September, 1984. 45 clergy were present, plus 3 laymen and 2 observers. After discussion and amendment the position was carried nem.con. with 2 abstentions.

1. We are deeply concerned:

(a) that the Archbishop of York and a significant number of the Bishops of the Church of England have recently, by word and action, declared as optional belief in the Virgin Birth of Jesus Christ and his Resurrection on the third day from the tomb.

(b) that such teaching is not compatible with the faith of the 'one, holy, catholic and apostolic church' nor the teaching of the Church of England as by law established.

(c) that such Bishops are calling into question the credibility and integrity of the Church of England; they are breaking the solemn oath of Canonical Obedience — the Canons being binding on Archbishops and Bishops as well as on the inferior clergy. Canon C.18.1 says:

> Every Bishop is to uphold sound and wholesome doctrine and to banish and drive away all erroneous and strange opinions.

And 'wholesome doctrine' is defined by Canon A.5:

> The Doctrine of the Church of England is grounded in the Holy Scriptures and in such of the teachings of the ancient fathers and councils of the Church as are agreeable to the said Scriptures. In particular such doctrine is to be found in the 39 Articles of Religion, the Book of Common Prayer and the Ordinal.

Legal advice reminds us that the Virgin Birth of Jesus Christ and especially his Resurrection on the third day from the tomb are positively affirmed in the authorities cited in Canon A.5.

(d) that the episcopate to which the clergy of the Church of England

221

can in conscience give allegiance is *only* the episcopate as it acts within the Church of England as by law established and therefore under Canon. Bishops defying the Canons can no longer *claim* canonical obedience themselves.

(e) that such Bishops are redefining 'Anglican Comprehensiveness' as a dialectic of mutually contradictory views. Thus it is possible for some to believe, and others not to believe that the remains of Jesus are still in the soil of Palestine. Both views, they maintain, witness to the truth. We are deeply disturbed not only because this is 'Gnostic' but also because such 'comprehensiveness', if generally accepted, would ultimately lead to the demise of the Church of England.

(f) that from our North Eastern perspective, the consecration of David Jenkins, by the Archbishop of York as Bishop of Durham, took place without a prior disclaimer of his controversial views on the Virgin Birth, the Resurrection and the New Testament. We are concerned too that the Bishop of Newcastle at his last Diocesan Synod, when speaking of the Virgin Birth and the Resurrection of Jesus Christ, said, 'We are allowed liberty of interpretation with regard to the sense in which they are true, whether they are true for instance, historically or theologically, or poetically or in analogical manner, or in more than one of these senses.' In simpler terms this says: 'belief in the historic fact of the Resurrection of Jesus Christ on the third day from the tomb, as clearly taught in the Bible, is optional.'

2. We are strongly convinced:

(a) that the urgent need in the North East is for local churches to be strengthened and to grow. The North East has witnessed a decline in church attendance over the last 100 years.

(b) that the clergy continually need renewed vision, confidence and hope in God and the Gospel of Jesus Christ. Denials of, or doubts over, fundamental doctrines by Bishops are demotivating.

(c) that new churches need to be planted in areas where the historic Christian faith has not penetrated. These may have to be 'alternative' churches unilaterally established. We should have as a goal, after research, a significant number of new 'worship centres' of at least 100 members each in the North East by 1990.

(d) that the current situation in society at large, evidenced by present violence and disagreement in our industrial sectors in the North East demonstrates a vacuum of spiritual values and spiritual direction in the Nation. Doubts, uncertainties and errors expressed by Bishops add to that vacuum. Our society, both rural and urban, desperately needs to hear the Gospel of Jesus Christ, who died and rose victorious over all the forces of evil and death on the third day. The recent visit of Dr Billy Graham to the North East has proved that there is sufficient responsiveness.

(e) that episcopal leadership is losing authority in the Church of England; a Bishop is a focus of unity only in so far as he is rooted in and proclaims the historic faith of the Christian Church. There is, nevertheless, always a need for a '3rd office' alongside that of 'presbyters' and 'deacons' to focus unity and provide encouragement; hence the seriousness of the present situation. Interim measures may be needed until there is a 'fully believing' bench of Bishops.

(f) that, thus, new forms of organization may have to be generated 'from the bottom'. A church so deeply divided in doctrine, embracing fundamentally opposed goals in mission and evangelism, cannot forever use common structures and finance. The structures and organizations of the Church are to promote commitment to the Gospel. Commitment to the Gospel is not to promote the survival of the structures and organization.

3. We necessarily conclude:

(a) that the goal of the growth of the local church for the spread of the Gospel of Jesus Christ should determine our priorities.

(b) that new initiatives should be taken to help the clergy of the North East in personal holiness, their ministry of teaching, preaching, worship, and also the practice of church growth, management and leadership; also that more ordinands and full-time workers should be recruited and trained.

(c) that to prevent any further confusion and to assist clarification, before a Bishop proceeds to conduct Confirmation, or exercise any other ministry in a local church, he could be asked to subscribe to the following declaration: *'I believe in the fact of the Virgin Birth of Jesus Christ and his Resurrection on the third day from the tomb as is clearly taught in the Holy Scriptures.'*

(d) that unity in programmes and structures should be fostered with all Anglican churches, of varying traditions, that can agree to the fundamentals of the faith, while at the same time being at liberty to disagree (strongly if necessary) over secondary matters. The fundamentals of the faith are the articles of the Apostles' and Nicene Creeds as interpreted by Scripture — these include the Resurrection of Jesus Christ on the third day from the tomb and the forgiveness of sins through justification by faith. At the appropriate time such unity should be extended to those Free Churches and Roman Catholic churches that agree to this basis.

(e) that freedom for theologians is carefully preserved, so that received opinions can be questioned. But there must be a boundary within which this takes place.

Appendix 2

The Anglican Evangelical Assembly

The following motion was passed overwhelmingly by the Anglican Evangelical Assembly on 4th January 1985. It said this:

This Assembly:

1. *recognizes* the responsibility of the Church in every generation to re-examine the historic Christian faith in the light of contemporary questioning and urges its members, out of concern for the truth, to be constructively involved in current theological debate.
2. *reaffirms* the biblical and credal doctrines
   (a) that the incarnation of Jesus was accomplished through an actual virgin conception, and
   (b) that the resurrection of Jesus from the dead was an event which included a bodily rising and resulted in an empty tomb on the third day.
3. *warmly commends* the paper produced by the Church of England Evangelical Council, entitled *A Statement about Jesus,* as a contribution to the current debate in the House of Bishops, the General Synod, and throughout the Church of England.
4. *deeply regrets* that the historical truth of the doctrines in paragraph 2 above has been denied or declared to be optional by some within the leadership of our church, thus causing widespread dismay.
5. *encourages* the House of Bishops to examine afresh the opportunities and constraints affecting the role of a bishop in teaching, defending and spreading the Catholic faith according to the Scriptures, and in being a focus of unity for the Church.
6. *urges* all churchmen who are, or could be, involved in the work of diocesan vacancy-in-see committees to ensure that commitment to biblical and credal orthodoxy is considered an essential criterion for candidates for episcopal office.